LEGAL FIRST AID
Your Quick Guide to Legal Action

Sunil Kumar Pathak

ISBN
Paperback 979-8-89498-361-5
Hardcase 979-8-89498-397-4

Disclaimer

Laws in India are continually changing with new amendments, rules, and court decisions. While I have taken great care to ensure that the information in this book is accurate and up-to-date at the time of writing, please be aware that legal provisions can evolve, and new interpretations may arise. If you notice any errors or outdated information, I encourage you to reach out, and I will strive to correct them in future editions. This book is intended to provide general legal information and insights. However, for any specific legal concerns or queries, it is always best to consult a lawyer or refer to the latest legal resources.

Thank you for your understanding, and I hope you find this book a useful and insightful resource.

Dedication

Babuji, Late Sh. Jagdish Pathak, and Ma, Late Smt. Shanti Devi, whose hard work, unconditional love, and dedication to making me an educated individual, will always inspire me in whatever I do. They did not just give me this life but also enshrined a continuing and never-ending courage to know more, irrespective of my mental or physical age. Throughout my childhood, they lovingly shared with me the verses of the esteemed poet Ramdhari Singh Dinkar. It was with the inspiration drawn from one such poem that I embarked on my journey from my hometown in Jharkhand to Delhi/NCR.

"Humko Samay ko Dekh Kar Nitya Chalna Chahiye

Badle hawa Jis tarah Humko Badlana Chahiye"

People who are not flexible in terms of time and situation just break like dead and dry wood unlike a fruit-laden green tree. You must understand the situation and act accordingly to survive. It is always best to be with change unless it's prima facie wrong.

This book, as well as my entire life, is devoted to my Ma and Babuji. It's a universal truth that the absence of your parents is felt more deeply when they are not by your side. I miss you, Ma and Babuji.

Through this book, I aim to honor one of their cherished aspirations: to assist others in any way possible at the time they need it most, as taught by our revered Maharishi Ved Vyas Ji.

"परोपकाराय पुण्याय पापाय परपीडनम्"

(Helping someone is the greatest deed, and causing pain to anyone is the worst sin)

I believe this book will serve as a guide for individuals navigating through crises that encompass personal, legal, financial, and social challenges, offering insights into the rights and protections given by Indian laws.

Contents

Foreword *11*

Preface *19*

Acknowledgement *23*

Introduction *25*

Common Cardinals Of Law *29*

SECTION 1: FEMALE **39**

Introduction – Protection under Bharatiya Nyaya Sanhita, 2023. The Immoral Traffic (Prevention) Act, 1956., The Dowry (Prohibition) Act, 1961., The Child Marriage Restraint Act, 1929., The Indecent Representation of Women (Prohibition) Act, 1986., The Commission of Sati (Prevention) Act, 1987., Protection of Women from Domestic Violence Act, 2005., The Sexual Harassment of Women at Workplace (Prevention, Prohibition and Redressal) Act, 2013.

1.1.   Kidnapping and Abduction 41

1.2.   Murder, Dowry Death, Abetment of Suicide 47

1.3.   Cruelty by Husband or His Relatives 53

1.4.   Unequal Opportunity of Employment 57

1.5.   Sexual Harassment 63

1.6.   Stalking 69

1.7.   Voyeurism 75

1.8.   Word, Gesture, or Act Intended to Insult the Modesty of a Woman . . . 81

1.9.   Disrobing a Woman 87

1.10. Human Trafficking 91

1.11. Acid Attack 95

1.12. Attempt to Commit Rape 99

1.13. Rape 103

SECTION 2: CHILDREN ...109

Introduction – protection under Bharatiya Nyaya Sanhita, 2023 erstwhile Indian Penal Code, 1860., Juvenile Justice Act, 2015., Information Technology Act, 2000., Protection of Child from Sexual Offenses Act, 2012.

2.1.   Children and the Indian Legal System ... 111

2.2.   Right of Survival - Health, Nutrition, Medication, and Home Care .. 115

2.3.   Right to Have a Family Environment, Love, and Trustful People Around ... 119

2.4.   Right to Have Parental Care and Fair Treatment of Parents ... 123

2.5.   Right to Education, Play, and Recreation ... 125

2.6.   Right to Be Protected Against Sexual Abuse and Exploitation ... 129

2.7.   Right Against Any Commercial/Economic Exploitation ... 133

2.8.   Right for Preferable Administration and Implementation of Child Rights ... 137

2.9.   Some Common Offenses Wherein One or Other Fundamental Right of Children is Violated ... 141

2.10.   Administration and Redressal of Child Rights ... 159

SECTION 3: GENERAL ...163

Introduction – Protection under Bharatiya Nyaya Sanhita, 2023 Erstwhile Indian Penal Code, 1860, and many other central & state laws, Information Technology Act, 2000., other special and allied laws. The reference of such Acts shall be mentioned in the specific offense and chapters.

3.1.   Abetment ... 165

3.2.   Attempt to Commit an Offense ... 169

3.3.   Criminal Breach of Trust ... 173

3.4.   Forgery and Cheating ... 177

3.5.   Corruption ... 181

3.6.   Criminal Trespass ... 185

3.7.   Hurt, Grievous Hurt, and Battery ... 191

3.8.   Theft, Robbery, and Extortion ... 197

3.9.   Marriage-Related Offenses ... 201

3.10. Criminal Intimidation 207

3.11. Public Nuisance & Misconduct By Intoxicated Persons 213

3.12. Recovery of Money and Bouncing of Cheque 219

3.13. Online Fraud and Cyber Crime. 225

3.14. Murder, Attempt to Murder & Culpable Homicide 233

3.15. Defamation, Slander, and Libel 239

3.16. Conspiracy 245

3.17. Sedition 251

3.18. Consumer Protection and Warranty. 257

3.19. Road Accident and Negligent Driving. 263

SECTION 4: MEN'S RIGHTS IN INDIA. 269

A brief thought on the specific right which are available or should be made available for men who suffers the misuse of strict and unilateral protection given to females under our legislature and judicial system.

Foreword

We often think that the law is only meant for the advocates, police, and the courts. This notion likely comes from the fact that understanding and interpreting the laws can be quite technical. There are multiple acts, rules, central and state laws, and even customary laws tied to specific societies or religions. The complexity increases with ambiguities in legislative drafting and varying interpretation by different courts.

But to genuinely benefit society, it's not just about having laws; we need proper enforcement through the police and courts. That's why I believe that basic legal education should be introduced in schools. Imagine having a generation of confident and well-informed young people who understand their rights and responsibilities.

The author, Sunil Pathak, recognized how difficult the law can be for everyday people and how it can sometimes be misused by enforcement agencies. He understands that our justice system is often more focused on hard evidence than on the real-life situations people face. He has truly decoded the complex legal landscape, making it easier for everyone to understand and take appropriate action.

Author's vision is to educate people, helping them stand up for their rights and make informed decisions—without overstepping others' rights or challenging the integrity of the country and governmental system. This book "Legal First Aid" is a product of that vision. Sunil avoids overcomplicating things and keeps his writing simple, lucid, conversational and relevant. At its core, the book is rooted in practical wisdom, compassion and driven by a deep desire to timely help the victims.

The book reflects Sunil's passion for empowering common people by raising awareness of their legal rights and making a meaningful impact through knowledge.

I wholeheartedly wish him all the best.

Dr. Kiran Bedi

Dr. Kiran Bedi

Dr. Kiran Bedi is a thought leader, known not only as India's first female IPS officer but also as a dedicated public servant and a compassionate human being. Over a career spanning more than four decades, she has been an inspiration in public administration, innovative policing, and meaningful prison reforms. Her unwavering commitment to integrity and positive social change earned her prestigious recognitions, including the Ramon  Magsaysay Award for government service and the Gallantry Award for acts of bravery.

She pursued her masters in political science from Punjab University, LLB from Delhi University and Ph.D. on drug abuse & domestic violence, from IIT Delhi. She broke new ground in 1972 by joining the Indian Police Service, taking on critical roles across Delhi. As the Inspector General of Prisons, she brought transformative reforms to Tihar Jail, tackling human rights abuses and introducing education and rehabilitation programs for inmates. Her commitment to change extended beyond borders, serving as the UN's first female Police Advisor to the Secretary-General in Peacekeeping Operations, representing India on global issues like crime prevention, drug abuse, and prison reform.

Outside her public service, Dr. Bedi is also an accomplished athlete, having been a National and Asian Tennis Champion. Her inspiring journey is captured in the biopic *Yes Madam, Sir*. She remains one of India's most trusted and admired figures, consistently rated highly in national opinion polls. Through her books, TV shows, and public speaking, Dr. Bedi continues to inspire and guide many. She has authored several insightful books including *It's Always Possible*, *What Went Wrong*, *As I See*, *Broom and*

Groom, and her autobiography *I Dare*. With her latest, *Fearless Governance*, drawing on her rich experiences as a top bureaucrat and Lieutenant Governor of Puducherry(2016-2021), and where she offers insights into leadership and governance.

Driven by her dedication to social service, she founded Navjyoti India Foundation and India Vision Foundation. For decades, these institutions have been helping underprivileged communities in rural and urban areas, and within prisons. Their work focuses on education, vocational training, healthcare, counseling, and skill-building, reaching thousands of underserved individuals, including prisoners and the children of police personnel.

Dr. Kiran Bedi's life is one of courage, compassion, and tireless service to mankind. She has dedicated her life to transparency, integrity, and the welfare of others, from pioneering prison reforms to advocating for the rights of the underprivileged. Her journey is a testament to the power of resilience and the impact one person can make through dedication and a genuine desire to serve. Like now, She will continue inspiring the future generations as well.

Foreword

Once in a while, life feels like a jigsaw puzzle with the pieces out of place. When everything feels upside down, you enter that phase where it seems impossible to face life head-on. You find yourself cornered, compromising, and accepting things simply because you didn't realize you had other choices.

And then, just once in a while, a book comes along that brings promise and hope—like a breath of fresh air. It shines a light on your rights, guiding you out of the dense jungle of uncertainty, helping you define your options, and offering the hope of something better. Suddenly, you feel empowered and more in control.

The author humbly calls this book "Legal First Aid" but it's far more comprehensive than that. It guides you through life's unexpected twists and turns, tackling difficult subjects head-on. Interpreting laws can be challenging; every comma, every word matters. But the way laws are interpreted also makes them fascinating. One court might rule one way, while another may interpret the same facts differently, sometimes even overturning the original judgment..

In this book, the author have deliberated critical legal topics, ranging from sexual offenses, abetment of suicide, and children's rights, to more daily issues like negligent driving, cheque bouncing, defamation, and public nuisance. He simplifies complex legal concepts and supports his analysis with data, offering a balanced view of laws and their enforcement.

The author sheds light on pressing issues like violence against women, including dowry deaths, sexual harassment and abetment of suicide, while highlighting how dowry remains a persistent problem in India. He also delves into the alarming fact of child's basic right violation and the fact that 50% of children under five die from malnutrition. The book further distinguishes between legal terms like dowry and stridhan, kidnapping and abduction, offering practical insights into laws that touch everyday life.

The book is not only timely but feels seasoned, drawing from practical wisdom. It offers a meaningful, practical dialogue, never bogging the reader down with unnecessary complexity. The writing is fresh, direct, and, most importantly, relevant. At its core, it is humane, driven by compassion and a desire for societal good.

What truly stands out is the man behind the book, Sunil Pathak, a thorough professional and a dear friend. Sunil is a law graduate from the University of Delhi and also affiliated with many esteemed institutions across globe. Sunil's commitment to empowering others goes far beyond his professional life. His philanthropic spirit is evident in his social work through Snehdhara Charity Council, dedicated to helping the underprivileged through food, education, and eco-friendly initiatives.

The book shows Sunil's deep dedication to social responsibility, as he endeavours to raise the social status of commoners and make a positive impact on society. If you're looking to change your narrative, switch tracks to reach a distant goal, or find light at the end of the tunnel, here is a book you can live your life by.

Adv. Shilpi Jain

Shilpi Jain

Renowned attorney at Supreme Court of India

Shilpi Jain's journey as a lawyer who is the first in her family is marked by determination, strength, and a strong dedication to justice. She completed her studies at Campus Law Centre, Delhi University and started her legal career in 1989. Beginning her career was a challenge due to societal doubt regarding her potential to excel in the legal industry, particularly given her sheltered up bringing in Dehradun. Soon  after, her commitment and enthusiasm for the legal field quieted those uncertainties. Recognized for her meticulous readiness and compelling persuasion, she promptly earned the admiration of her colleagues and the legal system.

In addition to her responsibilities in the courtroom, Shilpi is driven by a deep passion to assist those who are unable to assist themselves. She has accepted many pro bono cases, advocating for the rights of those in need. One of her most significant cases was when she represented a nurse who was a victim of rape in the Shanti Mukund case. She not only made sure that a First Information Report (FIR) was filed but also managed to get the hospital's license suspended for not giving appropriate care. In a different notable instance, she obtained a guilty verdict with in only 11 days for the sexual assault of a German woman in Rajasthan, even though the perpetrator was the son of a senior police officer. Her courage in handling such cases, despite facing threats, demonstrates her firm dedication to her clients.

Apart from her work as a lawyer, Shilpi is a recognized figure in the media. She is often cited in national newspapers and magazines, participates in television debates providing legal perspectives, and contributes articles on significant legal matters for prominent publications like *Hindustan Times*. She has had a broader influence, not limited to specific cases only, by playing a role in developing policy. This includes her effective advocacy for the Traders Association of India, ensuring their participation in talkson FDI policy.

Preface

During my legal education at Delhi University and on other occasions thereafter, I actively participated in moot courts, mediation and arbitration mocks, and youth parliament mocks, which aided in honing my legal skills. Additionally, I completed various internships and apprenticeship programs with non-governmental organizations, giving me the opportunity to help people obtain justice. The analysis of legal provisions, the legal position in society, and legal precedents are always the most important topics during formal education. However, when it comes to real life, we all enter an unfamiliar territory: the legal procedure. As a law student or even as a law graduate, there is very limited orientation to procedural laws. I was always very keen to understand how various aspects of law, including the complaints, police, prosecution, and courts function. Over time, I realized that procedural aspects occupy a paramount position and really define the outcome of a legal case. So, "How and when you do" is equally important to "what you do" during the preliminary case building, trial, and judgments.

I always felt a need for a book that could elaborate on the process of taking action against any wrongdoing, be it filing a simple complaint, FIR, investigation, or a comparatively extensive process of trial. Moreover, with evolving social scenarios, offense categories, victim profiling, etc., an easy interface about the life cycle of litigation from inception to conclusion is needed for every citizen who wants to know and protect their rights.

This book will help you navigate smoothly from complaint/preliminary investigation to trial, and by the end, you will have an aerial view of our country's legal topography as well. When a person understands the fundamentals of legal mechanisms, it becomes easy for even a professional lawyer to interact, explain, and clarify various legal nuances to the litigant.

Any legal case, more specifically a criminal case, depends a lot on facts like the timing of the police complaint, preservation, presentation, appreciation of evidence, and envisioning procedural aspects involved in a trial. Hence, I decided to write this book to address the needs of beginners and the precautions they should take to keep the litigation procedure and outcome in their favor.

Throughout this book, I have tried to focus on the procedural aspects of law. My focus is on the application of legal principles to factual scenarios in day-to-day life. For a better understanding of what to do when an event occurs, how the police record the complaint and investigate, and what is the procedure followed in court during trial and judgment, etc., I have categorized the most common offenses into categories like child, female, male, and general.

The book has been segmented in such a way that a particular category will find the following at one place:

- Legal provisions related to offenses that may be committed against them,

- Their rights related to the offense,

- Provisions, definitions, and punishments as per specific laws and The Bharatiya Nyaya Sanhita 2023, (erstwhile the Indian Penal Code 1860),

- The first few steps of the action they should take to make their case stronger.

- The judicial precedents they could refer to understand the court's stand

I intend for this book to become a "first aid kit" for you with respect to legal knowledge and basic procedures relating to a few common offenses, which must practically be known to you as a citizen of this country. My intention is not to turn you into a legal wizard or practitioner but to make a humble effort to bring awareness. This book cuts through the confusion and tells you exactly what information you need (the details) and conveniently puts it all in one place (where to find them) and also in a very lucid language, short sentences and conversational tone.

May you never face any breach of your rights, but knowledge is power! This book equips you to face any legal situation that might arise. I hope you enlighten yourself and help others too and this way you will help me to achieve my mission to disseminate the awareness of legal rights to commoners.

Acknowledgement

The journey of writing this book began in late 2021, during a time of significant anticipation in the legal community. The Honourable Home Minister had just hinted at upcoming changes to the IPC, CrPC, and the Indian Evidence Act. By January 2022, these hints became a formal announcement, and suggestions were being sought from Members of Parliament. Although I finished the draft by June 2022, I realized that referencing outdated provisions wouldn't serve future readers well. It became essential to balance the old laws with the newly enacted legislation, ensuring the book remained relevant and forward-looking.

This project has been a labor of love, requiring deep dives into research, countless brainstorming sessions, and invaluable discussions. I have relied heavily on a vast array of resources—bare acts, legal literature, articles, blogs, and research reports—contributed by numerous individuals and institutions, both within India and internationally. I am deeply grateful to everyone who contributed, even if they aren't mentioned by name. This book is a reflection of all your insights and knowledge.

I owe a special debt of gratitude to my colleagues and professional friends. I am particularly thankful to Adv. Mr. Rahul Kishore, whose experience in litigation—dealing with complainants, defendants, police, and the courts—brought clarity and depth to our discussions. His insights were invaluable in shaping many aspects of this book. I was also fortunate to have the guidance and encouragement of Justice Dinesh Kumar, District Judge in my hometown of Garhwa, Jharkhand, whose wisdom has been a constant source of inspiration.

I am also deeply appreciative of the unwavering support provided by my in-house counsel, Adv. Ms. Harshini Ramakrishnan. Her contributions to content design, research, and editing were instrumental in bringing this book to life. I want to extend my heartfelt thanks to Ms. Anshupriya Sen, Ms. Himanshi Garg, and Ms. Shreemayi Pathak for their diligent research support.

To my mentors, elders and friends—Puneet Pushkarna, Pankaj Sudan, Nikhel Kochhar, Braj Bihari Pandey, Neena Sen, Anil Pathak, Manav Mehra, Kaushal Mahaseth, Darshan Bhinde, Bhuvnesh Jangid, Rajesh Suri, Anant verma, Vipin Sharma, and Rishabh Pathak. Thank you for your invaluable insights, motivation and for generously sharing your time and experiences.

Finally, my deepest gratitude goes to my wife, Archna, and my children, Shreemayi and Shashwat. Their sacrifices of family time and their constant encouragement have been the bedrock of this project. This book is as much a testament to their support as it is to my efforts.

Introduction

As the famous maxim goes, "Ignorantia juris non excusat," which means that ignorance of the law is no excuse. This is where the complexity reaches the next level: for a person to get some relief/remedy/court order, they have to know it all. I understand that one may not be aware of all these laws, rules, and regulations, but knowing the fundamental and basic workings of the law does really help, and so this basic working knowledge is indispensable for every aware citizen of India.

Anything we do in society is somehow related to a legal framework. Entrepreneurship, marriage/live-in relationships, driving, trading of goods, personal or corporate services, etc., are all subject matters of law. It is difficult to escape from the ambit of law. Therefore, it is necessary to understand how our legal system works. If we are able to perceive the legal system from an aerial view, then zooming in or microscopic examination of complexities in various specialized branches of law will become uncomplicated for any literate individual.

Let me first brief you on India's legal system. As one of the Commonwealth countries, we follow the common law model prevalent in many other countries. The Constitution of India has set up 3 branches of the State:

1.	The executive,

2.	The judiciary,

3.	The legislature.

These branches are demarcated by their respective areas of jurisdiction. The judiciary is vested with the power to ensure that each branch of the Constitution operates within its constitutional boundaries. It is also the sole interpreter of the Constitution and the sole arbiter in all constitutional disputes.

The judicial hierarchy places the Supreme Court at the apex level. It adjudicates constitutional matters and also acts as the final court of appeal in certain civil and criminal matters. Each State has its own High Court, which serves as the ultimate appellate court. Invariably, all cases are first listed at district/local courts and then, moves to higher courts, depending on the nature, subject, financial value, and other factors.

The Constitution of India is the main law of the land and serves as the foundation of all laws and regulations. Just to give you a relevant glimpse of it and its functioning, let me elaborate a little.

The preamble of our Constitution itself secures for all its citizens:

- JUSTICE, social, economic, and political
- LIBERTY of thought, expression, belief, faith, and worship
- EQUALITY of status and opportunity; and to promote among them all
- FRATERNITY assuring the dignity of the individual and the unity and integrity of the Nation

The Indian Constitution provides for Fundamental Rights, Fundamental Duties, and Directive Principles of State Policy to regulate the conduct of citizens among themselves, as well as the state's conduct toward the citizens. These different chapters of the Indian Constitution provide a rulebook of rights, duties, and guidelines for citizens behavior and conduct, along with the parameters with which the government has to keep itself fully aligned while making laws.

The Fundamental Rights are defined as the basic human rights of all citizens of India for their peaceful co-existence. All these rights are enforceable by the courts, subject to specific restrictions. The basic idea behind formulating these Fundamental Rights is to protect the liberty of citizens and to maintain the social democracy of the country based on the factors of equality in society.

The Fundamental Duties have been defined as the moral obligations of all citizens to help promote the welfare of the country and to uphold the unity of the nation.

The Directive Principles of State Policy serve as directives to be incorporated by the government while framing laws. These principles are the fundamental guidelines for the State to apply in framing, enacting, and passing laws, and thereby establishing a social, economic, and democratic nation. Hence, the directive principles give the right to make laws and regulations, which in turn confer legal rights to citizens under these legislations. Numerous legislations, along with their underlying rules and regulations, often lead to complex scenarios for individuals, marking the beginning of legal complexities.

India follows the adversary system of legal procedure. This means that the judge acts as a neutral person, upholding the balance between the contending rivals without actively taking part in the forensic debate in the court. The parties involved in a case need to present their facts, evidence, witnesses, and other compliances to the court, which then decides based on those evidence and witnesses. Under these circumstances, the substance of the event, issues, basic and circumstantial facts, procedures, and regulations define the merit of a case and the enforcement of rights given under these legislations.

Despite appearing to be a lucid model of functioning, the legal system, including the judicial mechanism, has always remained complex for commoners, for the reasons mentioned above and the sheer number of legislations formulated and implemented by the government. It is a surprising fact that excluding all the laws enacted by state governments and the rules/regulations established under them, the central government alone has passed over 1,300 Acts since independence. A person facing a tragedy/crisis and wanting to exercise a legal right/remedy is often puzzled with a list of questions like:

- What are the applicable laws?
- Which is the appropriate authority to approach when making a complaint?
- Which lawyer is good and reliable?
- Who will draft the complaint/FIR and pleadings?
- What is the time limitation for making a complaint/filing an FIR?
- What is the court fee/procedures/dates/place?
- What if the government officer/police do not take any action?
- What if you get unfair/unequal treatment?

A person having their first exposure to legal issues might search the internet or ask a few friends and likely become confused about how to approach the situation in the most appropriate manner and what could help the victim make a strong case for a favorable judgment. Any relief sought before the court of law is decided in accordance with the laws of the land, which include substantive central/state acts, procedural laws, regulations, government orders, precedents, laws from the pre-independence era (for example, the Indian Penal Code from 1860), and often local/cultural customs as well.

With this book, I aim to suggest on many basic questions you may have, making you knowledgeable enough to refer to the appropriate law, regulation, forum, or court and take all possible precautions, in case some unforeseen crisis occurs in your life or in the lives of your friends or family.

May you benefit from the content of this book.

Thank you.

Common Cardinals Of Law

Frequently used and basic terms in law and the enforcement of rights are the most important aspects of this book, and you must understand them thoroughly. This will help you better understand the chapters of this book and analyze many other aspects related to offenses that may be committed against the state, person, property, goodwill, process, etc.

1. Civil Case and Criminal Case

Civil law is a general law that resolves disputes between 2 organizations or individuals. Under civil law, the offender will have to compensate the affected organization or individual if the liability is proved in court and the court directs so. Civil law generally deals with property, money, housing, divorce, custody of a child in the event of divorce, etc., so it is essentially an inter-party matter. In civil law cases, there is no punishment like in criminal law, but the aggrieved party receives compensation, and the dispute is settled.

On the other hand, criminal law deals with offenses committed against society. It specifies varying degrees of punishment in line with the seriousness of the crime committed. Criminal law addresses serious crimes such as murder, rape, arson/dacoity, robbery, assault, etc. The purpose of criminal law is to punish the offenders, protect society, and maintain law and order.

While you may go to court and file a suit for a civil matter, under criminal law, to start a case, a complainant needs to go to the police first, and the crime needs to be investigated by the police. Thereafter, a case can be filed in court by the police, and the court hears the matter. Finally, after the investigation and framing of charges, the trial of the case begins. In a criminal case, either the accused is found guilty or acquitted, and sometimes, the court may issue a warning or penalty if the allegation is not solely proven beyond a reasonable doubt.

2. Court of Jurisdiction

The term "jurisdiction" simply means the power to adjudicate and decide the matter in issue. The word is derived from combining 2 Latin words: "juris" (law) and "dicere" (to speak). Hence, jurisdiction refers to the power of courts to settle or speak on disputes. There are various sources of such jurisdiction, including:

1. Territorial Jurisdiction refers to a geographical area defined for a particular court.

2. Pecuniary Jurisdiction involves setting a monetary limit. For example a junior civil court judge's jurisdiction may be limited to cases involving amounts up to 300,000/ or otherwise.

3. Subject Jurisdiction pertains to the court's authority to hear specific types of cases, such as consumer courts handling disputes related to defective goods or deficient services. Exclusive Jurisdiction, such as contractual mentions of a particular court.

4. Appellate Jurisdiction, for example, a state High Court has appellate jurisdiction over all district courts.

5. Original Jurisdiction, for instance, a family court hears cases first on matrimonial matters.

6. Special Jurisdiction such as juvenile courts or economic offense courts.

7. Legal jurisdictions are provided by Constitution/Special Statutes, such as writ petitions, etc.

3. Cognizable and Non-Cognizable Offenses

Cognizable offenses are those in which the police can arrest the accused without a warrant. The police can also begin an investigation without the permission of the court. The accused is arrested and presented before the court within a stipulated time, which is within 24 hours. The First Information Report (F.I.R.) is registered by the police in the case of cognizable offenses only. When information is received regarding the commission of a non-cognizable offense, the police cannot initiate an investigation without the order of the appropriate jurisdictional magistrate.

In non-cognizable offenses, a police officer has no authority to arrest without a warrant. The Station House Officer (SHO)/Officer in Charge of the Police Station registers the substance of information in the form of a Non-Cognizable Report (NCR).

For instance, if a person causes simple hurt, it is considered a non-cognizable offense. However, if simple hurt is caused using a dangerous weapon or if grievous hurt is inflicted on the victim, the offense falls under the category of cognizable offenses, and an F.I.R. needs to be registered.

4. Bailable and Non-Bailable Offenses

Offenses are further classified as bailable and non-bailable offenses. In the case of cognizable and non-bailable offenses, the police/investigating officer has the discretion to arrest the accused/offender without needing to obtain warrants from the court. After the arrest, the accused/offender is produced before the court and may be granted regular bail by the court. This type of bail is called court bail. If bail is not granted, the accused is sent to judicial prison/jail.

For bailable offenses, the accused is apprehended by the police or investigating officer and granted bail at the police station itself. This occurs after the accused signs a bond and provides an undertaking to appear before either the investigating officer or the court at a later time. This is called police bail. Bail is closely linked to fundamental rights, and unless there is a compelling reason recorded by the police in their case diary, the police cannot reject bail in the case of bailable offenses.

5.   Compoundable and Non-Compoundable Offenses

Compoundable offenses are those where the complainant (the one who has filed the case, i.e., the victim) can enter into a compromise and agree to have the charges dropped against the accused. Section 359 of the Bharatiya Nagarik Suraksha Sanhita, 2023 (erstwhile 320 CrPC) lists such offenses as compoundable. The result of compounding is acquittal. For some offenses, like theft or grievous hurt, compounding is possible only before the court when the final report is filed. For simpler, inter-party offenses like adultery or defamation, compounding can be done without court permission.

Non-compoundable offenses are comparatively serious or grave and cannot be settled between parties. Because they are considered crime against the system and governance, the state becomes a party to the case rather than just the victim. Examples include murder, robbery, extortion, and dacoity.

6.   Public Interest Litigation (PIL)

Under Indian law, **PIL** means litigation for the protection of public interest. It is litigation introduced in a court of law not by the aggrieved party but by the court itself or by any other private party. It is not necessary for the person who is the victim to personally approach the court.

Public interest litigation is not defined in any act or legislation but is a power given to people at large through proactive judicial activism. Such cases may occur when the aggrieved party may not have the foresight or necessary resources to represent their concerns in court. Although the main and only focus of such litigation is public interest, there are various areas where a public interest litigation can be filed. For example:

- Violation of basic human rights/fundamental rights

- Improper functioning of government or public duty

- Any act or regulation that may be against the spirit of the constitution and national interest.

A PIL should be filed in a specific format, but the court may accept even a simple complaint or letter. Once a PIL has been filed, it cannot be subsequently withdrawn. The court may proceed suo- motu. These rules regarding PILs have been enunciated by the Supreme Court to ensure that PILs do not become a device to settle personal scores and that those initiating proceedings under a PIL do not have any vested interests. If personal litigation is filed under the guise of a PIL, the court may impose costs against such individuals.

7. Intention and Motive

In every criminal case, the intention of the offender is of foremost importance because guilt or innocence can only be proved with it. On the other hand, while motive may play a substantial role for investigating agencies, it does not play a significant role in determining guilt or innocence. Intention is the basic element for making a person liable for a crime, often confused with motive.

The primary difference between intention and motive is that intention specifically indicates the mental state of the accused and defines what's going on in their mind at the time of the commission of a crime, whereas motive implies the motivation, i.e., what drives a person to do or refrain from doing something.

No matter whether the act is committed with a good intent or a bad one. If a person does something purposefully and consciously (without any coercion and in sane minds), which is prohibited by the law, it will amount to criminal liability irrespective of his/her motive.

While intention determines whether the accused committed the crime purposely or accidentally, motive answers the question of why the accused committed the crime. Simply put, motive impels intention, so the latter arises out of the former.

8. Parties to a Legal Case

In a legal case, the plaintiff or complainant is the person who initiates the lawsuit. They are the ones who claim to have been wronged and seek a remedy from the court. These are complaining parties. More often, we use them interchangeably, but legally speaking, the plaintiff is used for civil matters, and the complainant is used for criminal cases. This is the only practical difference. In civil lawsuits, the plaintiff can also be the complainant; if not, then the complainant may or may not join the plaintiff in action against the defendant.

On the other hand, Defendants/Accused are the people against whom the suit/complaint is filed and who defend themselves. The person who files a criminal complaint alleging the commission of an offense is called the Complainant, and the opposite party is called the Accused.

In a criminal proceeding, when a complainant files a case, the state becomes the party and starts prosecuting the offender/accused, and this is why they are called the prosecutor. So, in all criminal cases, the complainant becomes a victim; the person who contests the case on behalf of the state becomes the prosecutor (PP- public prosecutor), and the offender in question becomes the Accused. Other nomenclature of these parties depends on the stage of the case, like:

- In Civil Suit - Plaintiff and Defendant
- In Criminal Proceedings - The Complainant (Victim) and Public Prosecutor (State) and the Accused

- In Appeal - The Appellant and Respondent

- In Petitions, including Writ petitions - The Petitioner and The Respondent

- In Court Order Executions - The Decree Holder (in whose favor the court has ruled) and the Judgment Debtor (Against whom the court has ruled)

9.   Lawyer, Advocates, Senior Advocate, and AOR

Lawyer and Advocate, these two words, even though used interchangeably, don't mean the same. You must understand the difference between the two before you hire one.

The term 'lawyer' is used to designate anyone in the legal profession, including a solicitor, barrister, and attorney. As compared to an advocate, they may have less experience. Having graduated from law school or having experience of only in litigations, they are yet to acquire the necessary experience and nuances needed to represent clients and get the verdict in their client's favor. However, they can appropriately be consulted for taking advice and making strategies around a case.

On the other hand, an advocate is a qualified individual who represents the client in a court of law, pleading for compensation or release depending on the nature of the case. After their education as law graduates, advocates shall have the necessary theoretical knowledge along with experience and skill in handling legal matters and procedures adopted by police and courts. They are heavily involved in representing their clients most of the time, and while pleading on their behalf, advocates try their utmost to get the favourable verdict for their clients.

The advocates are registered as legal professionals under the Indian Advocates Act 1961, and they need to abide by certain ethics, codes, and even dress. The Advocate Acts, lay out the legal framework for legal practitioners, as well as guidelines for the establishment of Bar Councils and an All India Bar. The advocates are invariably members of some or other bar councils and so they need to abide by some code of conducts.

Senior advocate is further recognition for their skills, experience, knowledge, and expertise. In general, it's granted by the Supreme Court or High Court on the basis of merit and seniority. Section 16 of the Advocates Act of 1961 states that there shall be 2 classes of advocates, namely, senior advocates and other advocates. The advocates, with their consent, may be designated as a senior advocate if the Supreme Court or a High Court is of the opinion that, by virtue of their ability, standing at the Bar, or special knowledge or experience in law, they deserve such distinction.

An Advocate on Record (AOR) is a distinguished class of legal practitioners within the Supreme Court of India. These advocates have successfully passed the examination administered by the Supreme Court and are duly registered as Advocates on Record with the esteemed Supreme Court of India.

So, while you may take advice on any matter from a lawyer on how to proceed, you will always need an advocate to represent your case in a court of law.

10. Writ Petitions

In order to protect the essential and fundamental rights given to every citizen under the Constitution of India, Articles 32 and 226 provide remedies and enforcement of these rights. Article 32 and Article 226 provide the right to move to the Supreme Court and the High Court, respectively, through appropriate proceedings. This right can be availed by any person whose fundamental rights are violated.

There are the following types of writs:

- Habeas Corpus filed against the illegal detention of an individual.

- Mandamus filed for instruction to a lower court/authority to do or abstain from doing something.

- Prohibition filed to prohibit a proceeding, stay an execution, or prevent another act.

- Certiorari filed to correct jurisdiction-related mistakes of an inferior court or tribunal.

- Quo Warranto is a court order filed to restrain a person from acting in the capacity of public office to which he/she is not entitled.

Both civil and criminal writ petitions can be filed in both the High Court and the Supreme Court under Article 226 and Article 32 of the Constitution, respectively. The stepwise procedure for filing a petition at both the High Court and Supreme Court is as follows:

- Draft writ petition – You must take the help of an expert for this.

- File the petition at the filing counter in court with the court fee.

- On the date of the hearing, the court will either reject or admit the petition and send a notice to the other party.

Then, the court will fix another date for the hearing. This will be in the presence of such other party if it chooses to appear, and the court will finally consider all the contents of the petition, thereby granting relief accordingly on the same date or the next.

The writ petition should be accompanied by an affidavit of the petitioner, duly sworn, along with the applicable court fee and all relevant documents on which the application is based.

SECTION 1

FEMALE

Introduction – Protection under **Bharatiya Nyaya Sanhita**, 2023. The Immoral Traffic (Prevention) Act, 1956., The Dowry (Prohibition) Act, 1961., The Child Marriage Restraint Act, 1929., The Indecent Representation of Women (Prohibition) Act, 1986., The Commission of Sati (Prevention) Act, 1987., Protection of Women from Domestic Violence Act, 2005., The Sexual Harassment of Women at Workplace (Prevention, Prohibition and Redressal) Act, 2013.

Kidnapping and Abduction

In India, Omni vans and the phrase "don't talk to a stranger" are reminiscent of the crimes of kidnapping and abduction. However, one cannot take these incidents lightly.

Before legally understanding how one can safeguard oneself from the crime, we need to understand the crime itself. It is apparently well-known to everyone. Kidnapping and abduction may be used together or interchangeably, but they are slightly different from each other. It is crucial to file a complaint accurately and specifically against the crime committed to ensure effective legal action. This is especially important as a lack of awareness can sometimes be exploited by authorities to prematurely close the case or downplay its severity. The word "kidnap" is formed from the combination of *"kid"* + *"nap,"* i.e., taking away a kid, which over the years has included adults in its periphery of meaning. Abduction, on the other hand, is when a person is taken by another through fraud or manipulation. The former is generally done for ransom money and the latter for other purposes. It is interesting to read further how men and women are abducted for vastly different reasons.

In India, Section 137 to 146 of The BNS, 2023 (erstwhile Indian Penal Code 1860, sections 359 to 374) cover various situations of kidnapping and abduction, and primarily these are crimes against kids and women.

However, the applicable laws apply to all irrespective of gender and age. What may be relevant for a female shall be applicable to a male victim, too, unless otherwise mentioned and differentiated.

According to the Bhartiya Nyaya Sanhita 2023, or erstwhile Indian Penal Code 1860, kidnapping is defined as the act of abducting or forcibly carrying away a person without his/her consent. Abduction, on the other hand, is defined as the act of forcibly taking away a person from his/her lawful guardian.

However, if the kidnapping or abduction is committed with the intention of murdering the person, the punishment is life imprisonment or death. If the person kidnapped or abducted is under 16 years of age, the punishment is more severe and can extend up to life imprisonment.

Section 137 of BNS 2023, or erstwhile Section 359 of IPC of 1860, mentions 2 forms of kidnapping:

- First, kidnapping from India, and
- Secondly, kidnapping from lawful guardianship.

Section 137 (a) or erstwhile Section 360 of IPC of 1860 defines kidnapping from India as: "Whoever conveys any person beyond the limits of India without the consent of that person, or of some person legally authorized to consent on behalf of that person, is said to kidnap that person from India," and **Section 137 (b) or 361 of erstwhile IPC** defines kidnapping from lawful guardianship, which primarily applies to minors and includes even enticing of children where force may not be used.

Section 138 of BNS 2023, or erstwhile Section 362 of IPC 1860, defines abduction as: "Whoever by force compels, or by any deceitful means induces, any person to go from any place, is said to abduct that person."

Section 138 of BNS, or erstwhile section 362 of IPC 1860, says that abduction can happen in 2 ways and one of which involves the usage of force to unsettle a person. In abduction, a person is forced to go from one place to another against his/her will. The use of force, as mentioned in this section, must be actual and not just a threat of force to constitute abduction. This chapter is fairly centered around the abduction of women for unlawful purposes.

According to the National Crime Records Bureau (NCRB) report, the driving forces behind kidnappings have been divided into 18 distinct categories, including murder, revenge, and marriage.

In 2021, 10,235 women were taken away for marriage. In 2016, 174,021 women went missing, which only increased in 2018 to 223,621. The state of Uttar Pradesh reported the maximum number of persons kidnapped and abducted, with 13,548. It is worrisome that only 52.9% of females could be saved.

The crime of abduction is a slippery road. The perpetrator may manipulate the case by wrongfully presenting the situation. In one instance, Lata Singh was an adult when she left her family to tie the nuptial knot with a man from a lower caste. Her brothers, who were unhappy with the alliance, filed a missing person report and alleged that Lata had been abducted. This resulted in the arrest of 3 people from her husband's family. In another instance, Dipti Sarna, an employee of Snapdeal, was abducted for the very purpose of marriage. For abduction to be completed, it is essential that the person is compelled to go from one place to another, either forcefully or by using deceitful means. It cannot be called abduction if the person is not taken to some other place.

The punishment for abduction vary depending upon the intent behind such crime and hence, one needs to know the specific punishments, prescribed under the Bhartiya Nyaya Sanhita 2023 (erstwhile Indian Penal Code 1860) and how to effectively use them in legal proceedings:

- Abducting with the intent of murder is punishable by imprisonment for life or rigorous imprisonment for a term that may extend to 10 years, and shall also be liable to fine, as per section 140 of BNS 2023 or section 364 of erstwhile IPC 1860.

- Forceful confinement of a person under section 142 of BNS 2023 or erstwhile section 365 of IPC 1860 can get the abductor punished as if they have committed the crime with same intent, as the actual accused.

- If a woman is coerced into marriage or illicit intercourse, the enforcer can be punished for up to 10 years along with fine under section 87 of BNS 2023 or section 366 of erstwhile IPC 1860.

- Abduction of a person and threatening the person to cause death or hurt, or by his conduct giving rise to a reasonable apprehension that such person may be put to death or hurt, or causing hurt or death to such person in order to compel the Government or any foreign State or international inter-governmental organization or any other person to do or abstain from doing any act or to pay a ransom, shall be punishable with death, or imprisonment for life, and shall also be liable to fine.

- According to section 140(3) of BNS 2023 or erstwhile section 365 of the Indian Penal Code 1860, abduction of any person with intent to cause that person to be secretly and wrongfully confined, shall be punished with imprisonment of either description for a term which may extend to 7 years, and shall also be liable to fine.

- Abduction of any person in order that such person may be subjected, or may be so disposed of as to be put in danger of being subjected to grievous hurt, slavery, or the unnatural lust of any person, or knowing it to be likely that such person will be so subjected or disposed of, shall be punished with imprisonment of either description for a term which may extend to 10 years, and shall also be liable to fine according to section 140(4) of BNS 2023 or erstwhile section 367 of IPC 1860.

- Whoever, knowing that any person abducted, wrongfully conceals or confines such person, shall be punished in the same manner as if he had abducted such person with the same intention or knowledge, or for the same purpose as that with or for which he conceals or detains such person in confinement.

- The concealment of the knowledge of such crime taking place is also a punishable offense, for which he/she/others will be treated the same as the kidnapper in the eyes of the law.

In general, these offenses are cognizable, non-bailable, and non-compoundable.

There is no easy solution to this serious crime. Considering the purpose of the abductor, it is only advisable to be always alert and on the lookout. Learning enough self-defence to face such unforeseeable circumstances is necessary.

Kidnapping and abduction are acts against the liberty of victims, especially women and children. There is a dire need to prevent these horrendous crimes and stop the culture of kidnapping and abduction from spreading, especially when it is done for marriages, forced sexual intercourse, forced begging, etc.

To overcome these offenses, not only do the government and police need to work together, but so do all common people. What is required to prevent these offenses is the joint effort of non-governmental organizations and government bodies and more awareness among the people at large. Apart from this, one should also take care of themselves by:

- Staying vigilant
- Avoiding risk area primarily during night
- Keeping family and friends aware of your whereabout
- Choosing safe transport to commute
- Carry safety tools such as pepper spray
- Set SOS in your phone
- Learn some self-defence practices like Judo/Martial art.

Always trust your instinct and if something doesn't feel right, then it probably isn't. May you never face this but if you get to see this then be brave enough to leave the trace, maintain calm and create rapport with abductor. Remember, this is a temporary situation, and your safety is the priority.

Murder, Dowry Death, Abetment of Suicide

This topic has been covered in Bhartiya Nyaya Sanhita 2023 (It was also present under erstwhile Chapter 16 of IPC of offences affecting the human body), which makes up 30% of total crime in India. Though Dowry deaths have shown a slow decline over the past 3 years, the abetment of suicide, in contrast, seen a substantial rise and accounts for 0.3% of total crime. In many cases, these two issues are interrelated, with appeals in courts being made on both charges against the offender.

Relatively, awareness of dowry cases has been decent in our country, whereas abetment of suicide is a complex crime needing our attention. It's difficult to get accurate and up-to-date data on dowry deaths worldwide, as these crimes are often underreported and misclassified. However, based on 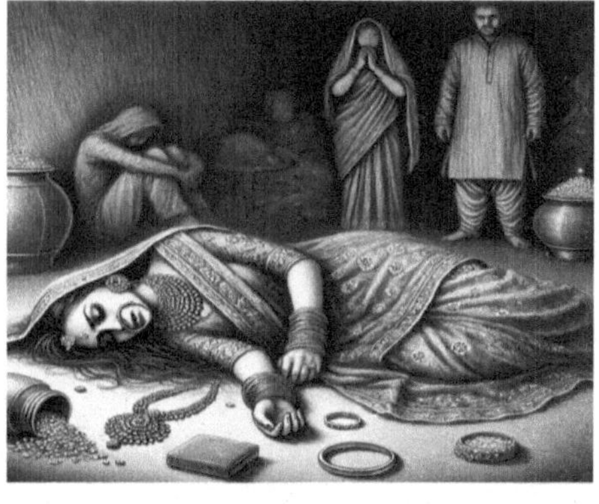 available data, it's estimated that dowry-related violence affects millions of women and their families around the world.

In India, according to the National Crime Records Bureau (NCRB), there were 7,304 reported cases of dowry deaths in the country in 2019 (In 2023, it is estimated that the reported crime of dowery death is 6450). Though certainly, there is decline in the incidences, however, the actual number is likely much higher, as many cases go unreported or are misclassified as accidents or suicides.

People are becoming more aware and vocal about dowry atrocities with growing exposure to media, which has sensitized the issue on several platforms. Many remember the episode of Satyamev-Jayate on Star Plus, which dedicated the whole episode to making people conscious of such heinous crimes. The efforts of NGOs and women's groups have further worked for the cause. What is not known to people is that the crime, which has been normalized as a customary ritual, has morphed from a token of love to greed.

Manu Smriti has mentioned the difference between dowry and bride's wealth. The term "Stridhan" has been floating since ancient times, which was the money given to the girl after marriage by her family to use as she likes. But with the advent of the British Raj, the anti-feminist law prohibiting women from possessing any property gave men the opportunity to make them dependent on male fraternity. In the time frame where a token of love turned into a form of extortion, a lot of lives have been lost, either due to the killing of the bride or forcing her to commit suicide.

The recognition of this crime finally took place when the first legislation came 14 years after independence in the form of The Dowry Prohibition Act, 1961, with 2 amendments in the same year. Both the offence of dowry murder and abetment of suicide often stem from similar patterns of abuse, but the critical difference lies in the ultimate outcome—murder involves an external act of killing, whereas abetment of suicide involves driving the victim to take her own life.

Abetment of Suicide is an act to encourage another person to commit suicide, creating an environment of dread and torture in which the aggrieved person is driven to take their own life. This was brought into the spotlight in the recent suicide case of Sushant Singh Rajput. Bhartiya Nyaya Sanhita 2023 under section 45 or the erstwhile IPC 1860 under section 107, defines abetment as:

- Abetment of a thing. —A person abets the doing of a thing, who—

- First. —Instigates any person to do that thing or

- Secondly. —Engages with one or more other persons in any conspiracy for the doing of that thing, if an act or illegal omission takes place in pursuance of that conspiracy, and in order to the doing of that thing; or

- Thirdly. —Intentionally aids, by any act or illegal omission, the doing of that thing.

Explanation 1. —A person who, by wilful misrepresentation or by wilful concealment of a material fact which he is bound to disclose, voluntarily causes or procures, or attempts to cause or procure, a thing to be done, is said to instigate the doing of that thing.

The reason these 2 crimes are related is because of the physical proximity of the offender and the sufferer. The former is strictly related to the family of the groom within the household, and the latter is not possible without the constant heated situation around the victim, which requires a consistent presence and coercing.

In the case of **Satbir Singh v. The State of Haryana**, Satbir, the accused, and his brother were sentenced to jail for 7 years as his wife set herself on fire just one year after their marriage. The father of the deceased received the news of his daughter attempting suicide by burning herself. By the time he made it to the hospital, his daughter had died. The aggrieved father lodged an FIR under Sections 304B and 306, IPC and the court upheld the conviction under section 304B for dowry death..

The act of dowry has not been defined under the Bhartiya Nyaya Sanhita 2023 or the erstwhile IPC 1860, but Section 80 (quondam Section 304 B) comes within the wider purview of Section 2(1) of The Dowry Prohibition Act, 1961.

Section 80 of BNS 2023 states:

- Death should be due to some bodily harm, just like in the case of Satbir Singh, where the bride died of burns.

- The death should be within the first 7 years of marriage.

- The bride has been tortured by the relatives of the accused.

- This death takes place soon in relation to the demand for dowry. Here, soon doesn't mean immediate but a reasonable proximity.

The laws for the said crime have been in place for more than 50 years, yet their implementation is lacklustre. It is important to be aware of the preventive/punitive measures prescribed to help you:

1. Section 103 of BNS 2023 (quondam 302 of IPC 1860): Punishment for murder. —Whoever commits murder shall be punished with death or imprisonment for life and shall also be liable to a fine.

2. Section 80 of BNS 2023 (quondam 304 B of IPC 1860): Dowry death.—(1) Where the death of a woman is caused by any burns or bodily injury or occurs otherwise than under normal circumstances within 7 years of her marriage, and it is shown that soon before her death, she was subjected to cruelty or harassment by her husband or any relative of her husband in connection with any demand for dowry, such death shall be called "dowry death," and such husband or relative shall be deemed to have caused her death.

3. Section 80 (2) of BNS 2023 states that whoever commits dowry death shall be punished with imprisonment for a term which shall not be less than 7 years but which may extend to imprisonment for life.

4. Section 108 of BNS (quondam 306 of IPC 1860): Abetment of suicide. —If any person commits suicide, whoever abets the commission of such suicide shall be punished with imprisonment of

either description for a term which may extend to 10 years and shall also be liable to a fine.

The Indian government has implemented several measures to address the issue of violence against women, including dowry deaths. For example, Nyaya Sanhita 2023 includes specific provisions to address dowry deaths and harassment of women, including Section 85 (quondam 498 A of IPC 1860), which criminalizes cruelty by a husband or his relatives against a married woman. Additionally, the government has also implemented awareness campaigns and programs to educate the public about the harmful effects of dowry and the importance of respecting women's rights.

The provisions under Section 80 of Bhartiya Nyaya Sanhita 2023 (quondam 304B of IPC 1860) are more stringent than those provided under Section 85 of Bhartiya Nyaya Sanhita (quondam 498 A of IPC 1860). The offense is cognizable, non-bailable, and triable by a court of Sessions.

Sections 194 and 196 of Bhartiya Nagarik Suraksha Sanhita 2023 (formerly addressed under Sections 174 and 176 of the Code of Criminal Procedure 1973) deal with cases of unnatural death. The Bhartiya Sakshya Adhiniyam 2023 (quondam The Indian Evidence Act 1872) has inserted a provision u/s 118 (erstwhile Section 113 B of The Indian Evidence Act 1872) for the cases of dowry deaths to form a presumption that the crime has taken place even if proper evidence is not available if there are grounds of some facts of dowry involved and the death is within the first 7 years of marriage.

It's important for individuals, communities, and the government to work together to address this issue and promote gender equality. Dowry deaths remain a significant problem in India and are a manifestation of the deep-seated social and cultural norms that perpetuate gender discrimination and violence against women. The government and civil society organizations are working to address the issue and eliminate this practice and protect the rights of women. However, despite these measures, violence against women and dowry-related deaths continue to be major issue in India, and much more needs to be done to eliminate these practices and ensure the safety and protection of women in the country.

Cruelty by Husband or His Relatives

The condition of women behind closed doors in India has been an open secret. It is an age-old mindset that has not yet freed itself and probably won't for the next 100 years. In light of this, it is evident that women face not just mental but also physical torture at the hands of their husbands and husband's families.

Domestic violence can be defined as "violent or aggressive behaviour within the home, typically involving the violent abuse of a spouse or partner." Domestic violence is a subset of violence against women and It is quite prevalent in India, as Indian society is defined by certain norms and

ritual practices that might be considered regressive. The dowry system is a glaring example of such a regressive practice and is considered one of the root causes of domestic violence in India.

The whole concept of a successful marriage is often defined by the amount of dowry the bride brings. If the girl's family is unable to fulfill this demand, then the whole cycle of additional dowry demands and domestic violence ensues. Regular beatings, deprivation of basic needs, emotional abuse like continuous demands for dowry, and insults to the woman and her family—this cycle keeps increasing every passing day. In most instances, the victim remains silent to avoid further distress and to protect her family. Financial dependence on her in-laws, lack of education and knowledge of her rights, and fear of social stigma also contribute to this silence. Often, these cases only reach the police or court when the victim either dies due to injuries, commits suicide, or is taken to the hospital for treatment.

Multiple commercial movies centered around this topic existed long before Section 498A (cruelty) was inserted into the IPC in 1983.

Section 85 and 86 of the Bhartiya Nyaya Sanhita 2023 (quondam Section498A of the Indian Penal Code 1860) defines the offense and punishment as follows:

"Whoever, being the husband or the relative of the husband of a woman, subjects such woman to cruelty shall be punished with imprisonment for a term which may extend to 3 years and shall also be liable to a fine."

Explanation.—

For the purposes of this section, "cruelty" as per Section 86 of the Bharatiya Nyaya Sanhita 2023 (quondam Section498A of the IPC 1860) means—

(a) any willful conduct which is of such a nature as is likely to drive the woman to commit suicide or to cause grave injury or danger to life, limb, or health (whether mental or physical) of the woman; or

(b) harassment of the woman where such harassment is with a view to coercing her or any person related to her to meet any unlawful demand for any property or valuable security, or is on account of failure by her or any person related to her to meet such demand.

Section 85 of BNS 2023 (quondam Section498A of the IPC 1860) has the following characteristics:

1. **Cognizable:** where the police can arrest without a warrant. Law enforcement has an obligation to report and investigate any crime that meets the legal definition.

2. **Non-bailable:** If a complaint is lodged under Section 498A, the magistrate can refuse bail and send the accused to judicial or police custody without the need for a bail hearing.

3. **Non-compoundable:** A petitioner cannot withdraw from a non-compoundable case, i.e., cannot settle outside court.

The act of domestic violence toward women is a human rights violation as well as an illegal act under Indian law, which has been formulated to ensure that all citizens are provided safety and security to live a life of freedom, dignity, and respect.

Article 15 of the Constitution of India and international conventions like the Convention for the Elimination of All Forms of Discrimination Against Women (CEDAW), which India has ratified, recognize women's unequal status and, therefore, make special provisions for women to address this inequality. Cases of cruelty have only been on the rise, with 136,234 cases in 2021 compared to 111,549 in 2020.

In India, domestic violence is governed by the Protection of Women from Domestic Violence Act 2005, and it is defined under Section 3, which states that any act, commission, omission, or conduct of a person that harms, injures or endangers the health or safety of an individual, whether mentally or physically, amounts to domestic violence. The Act also mandates the appointment of a protection officer, whose main role is to administer and take appropriate action to protect the people covered under the Act. The Act is not for women alone but also for children, the elderly, and other specially-abled people whose rights may be violated by someone stronger. The Protection of Women from Domestic Violence Act, 2005 also has provisions under which one can file complaints for cruelty related to dowry. This cruelty does not necessarily mean physical abuse; mental torture can lead a victim to the cusp of depression and force them to end their life.

The existing hesitancy among victims of domestic violence to turn to the law for such crimes is slowly changing. Domestic violence was often not handled as a legitimate crime but instead as a family matter, negating the rights of women as citizens.

With increasing awareness of Section 85 and 86 of the Bharatiya Nyaya Sanhita 2023, there may not be a decrease in the number of domestic violence cases, but the reporting and action taken against the perpetrators will hopefully increase. Hope the trend changes and we work towards fostering the respect for a married woman as daughter, wife, mother and home maker.

Unequal Opportunity of Employment

In 2005, Rajendra Gupta and other male cabin crew members of Air India (pre-1997 batch) filed a petition against the administrative decision of Air India to give equal rights to female cabin crew to become Flight Supervisors (IFS), a position previously reserved for males. Why? The argument given was that the position of IFS was "superior" and that male crew members couldn't perform their functions under the supervision of a female IFS. They argued that at least 50% of the seats should be reserved for male crew members.

The court quashed the appeal and merged the cadres, ruling that the 2 different cadres were unnecessary and violated Article 14 of the Indian Constitution. This case occurred 15 years ago, and the work culture has been shifting since then. The development of the tech industry has given women a chance

at equality, yet 85% of women in India believe they have not received a promotion due to their gender. More than half of working women feel they have faced gender discrimination at work. More than 7 out of 10 women feel that family duties hinder their career success.

We have discussed the slowly progressing state of women, and it is reflected in the working ecosystem as well. Women are still not given equal opportunities and In fact, after the pandemic, one of the most adversely affected groups in terms of employment was women in India.

The prejudice of women as a "thing of beauty," a "fragile flower," or "too naive" has clouded the mindset of employers, despite this modern era, where technology has taken over many roles, necessitating someone in charge who can handle the technology. This modern era is all about mental and cerebral competency, for which women are at par with men and even superior at times. The 10th and 12th Results every year, very well indicates towards this superior mental competence of female students.

No matter how much we segregate science, commerce, and arts, the practical aspect of commerce and generating wealth has always, either bolstered or sabotaged by prevailing sociological perspective within the society. Even with a fast-growing service sector and more opportunities for women, they have only been able to contribute 18% to the GDP. To our surprise, In urban cities, women are less engaged in the workforce than their rural counterparts. Look at villages and mountains areas of India, where you will find the female of family working more than their male counterparts.

The unwelcoming work environment is one of the leading factors in women opting out or, worse, not joining the urban workforce. Prime examples can be seen in job descriptions and interviews, where women are judged based on their communication skills and physical appearance, while men are typically evaluated basis their problem-solving ability.

Women must know they are protected under several rights provided by the Constitution and corporate laws. During their employment, all workers are entitled to certain rights and duties. These rights safeguard employees from discrimination based on religion, race, caste, or gender, protecting their interests and even the right to privacy. Certain rights as a worker/female worker are as follows:

- **Right to complain or protest about work:** Every employee has the right to complain about working conditions, as provided under the Factories Act 1948. It also provides that every worker has the right to object and protest against unacceptable working conditions.

- **Right to equal pay for equal work:** An organization where workers in the same position do the same work cannot have discriminatory pay scales under the Equal Remuneration Act, 1976. Equal pay relates not only to basic pay but also includes other benefits and allowances. There should not be any discrimination while paying employees based on their gender, caste, creed, etc. Even our Constitution under Article 39 ensures the equal pay for all the citizens irrespective of gender, religion, caste, creed etc..

- **Equal opportunity to work:** Section 5 of the Equal Remuneration Act, 1978, talks about providing the same platform as men for women to work, not just when they are offered the job but at different stages, including promotion. Article 16 of the Constitution mentions the same in terms of government jobs.

- **Right to have leave:** Every worker in an establishment is entitled to leave when needed, and in the case of sick leave beyond certain days, a worker must submit medical certificates.

- **Right to timely salary:** Workers are entitled to receive a timely salary at the end of every month. This encourages workers to work harder, protects their rights, and maintains a sense of security, as most depend on their salary to run their households.

- **Right to maternity benefits:** All women employees are provided with rights and benefits related to maternity, helping them maintain a balanced family and work life. A woman can claim maternity benefits upon completing 80 days of employment and is entitled to 26 weeks' leave under the Maternity Benefit Act of 1961, which was amended in 2017.

Protection under the Constitution - Articles 14 & 15 cover the ambit of the right to equality. Article 14 states, "Equality before law.—The State shall not deny to any person equality before the law or the equal protection of the laws within the territory of India." Article 15 prohibits discrimination on grounds of religion, race, caste, sex, or place of birth.

What to Do If You Are Wrongfully Terminated:

Once you have established the reason for wrongful termination, you can choose the appropriate legal remedy against your company. Here's a guide on what you can do against the illegal termination of employment:

Start by writing a formal complaint or grievance letter for wrongful termination to your company's Human Resources (HR) Department. Give them time to evaluate the case and provide a proper response. HR can often resolve disputes with the employer and halt the termination. If the HR department's responses are unsatisfactory, hire a lawyer specializing in labor laws and send a legal notice to the employer detailing the case and seeking end-to-end damages. These damages may include:

- Back pay
- Lost benefits
- Out-of-pocket losses
- Injunctive relief
- Punitive damages
- Severance package
- Retrenchment compensation
- Health insurance
- Provident fund

In the case of a contractual agreement violation, you can file a lawsuit against the employer for wrongful termination in the Labor Court or even a civil court for violation of terms of employment agreement. The court can order the employer to reinstate you in your job and pay damages for wrongful termination.

Our government is helping women take charge and become the face of Indian economy with schemes like Stand Up India for loans, Mahila e-Haat (an online platform for women to sell their products), the Support to Training and Employment Program for Women (STEP) Scheme to help women learn skills for self-employment, and the Women Entrepreneurship Platform (WEP), a scheme by NITI Aayog to support women entrepreneurs.

The pandemic has increased the gender gap by 4.3%, discouraging women from the workforce. To help and support each other, women should be informed about government schemes and their rights. Women were respected and known for their intelligence and Gargi, Sati Anusuiya, Ghosha, and Maitreyi are just examples. Industrialization and the use of heavy machinery that required physical strength downplayed the capabilities of women, which at least can now be restored in this modern era of technology wherein mental competency has taken over physical muscles.

Sexual Harassment

Sexual harassment is an umbrella term used to describe sexual discrimination and unwanted sexual advances. The term was coined in the U.S. in the early 1970s. Generally, sexual harassment falls into 3 categories:

1. Sexual Coercion - Demanding sexual favors in return for something, such as sustaining in the workplace.

2. Unwanted Sexual Attention - This includes the most common and prevalent form of undesirable sexual behavior, which is non-consensual, including unwanted touching, stroking, hugging, groping, kissing, and asking for dates. Unwanted sexual attention is an all pervasive word and can include even sexual assault and rape.

3. Gender Harassment - Here, gender determines discriminatory attitudes, generally against women. This type is not related to sexual advances but to sexism. It is often overlooked as a form of sexual harassment. The biased preference for men over women in certain tasks and positions, often exemplified by derogatory terms like calling women 'cunts' or men 'pussies,' reflects deeply ingrained sexism. These contemptuous remarks perpetuate harmful stereotypes, suggesting that women are ill-suited for leadership roles and that men have no place in childcare.

In a patriarchal society where women have often seen themselves as a second sex, it is essential to understand that the Constitution provides them with rights to address these distinctions between males and females. Recognizing that sexual harassment has existed since the first crime committed against a woman is crucial. The shame felt by women to the extent that they accept this as part of being a woman is dangerous for a society that has recently begun to relax its orthodox constraints. Women need to remember that such acts infringe on their fundamental rights as provided under following Articles

1. Article 14 of the Constitution, which identifies sexual harassment as a violation of the fundamental right of a woman to equality.

2. Discrimination on grounds of religion, race, caste, gender, or place of birth is prohibited under Article 15.

3. Under Article 21, which talks about the right to life and living with dignity, sexual harassment is a violation of this right.

Our constitution and other laws has provided us with a system that can help us in filing complaints.

In India, Section 75 (1) of Bharatiya Nyaya Sanhita 2023 (Quondam Section 354A of the IPC 1860) defines sexual harassment as a man committing any of the following acts—

(i) physical contact and advances involving unwelcome and explicit sexual overtures; or

(ii) a demand or request for sexual favors; or

(iii) showing pornography against the will of a woman; or

(iv) making sexually colored remarks,

    shall be guilty of the offense of sexual harassment.

Punishment (Section 75(2) and 75 (3) of the BNS 2023 or erstwhile Section 354A of the IPC 1860):

Any man who commits the offense specified in clauses (i), (ii), or (iii) above shall be punished with rigorous imprisonment for a term which may extend to 3 years, with a fine, or with both. Any man who commits the offense specified in clause (iv) of subsection (1) shall be punished with imprisonment of either description for a term which may extend to one year, with a fine, or with both.

You need to remember that it's not your fault. No matter what the harasser might say, there's no such thing as "asking for it." You have a right to feel safe. If any act or comment makes you feel stressed, depressed, anxious, or losing sleep, talk with a friend, therapist or counsellor. They can help you find ways to cope and recover from stress. Sexual harassment and its development in the workplace go hand in hand as the awareness of misconduct in the workplace came into the center stage at the same time the term sexual harassment was formed. Countless women have come to the forefront and talked about their experiences in the workplace.

In India, this was brought to light in the late '90s when Bhanwari Devi, who worked as a saathi (friend) for the state government's Women's Development Program (WDP) since 1985, was gang-raped by upper-caste men for preventing an eleven-month-old girl from getting married. Unfortunately, she never got justice and was ostracized from her own village for false allegations. This slowly caught the attention of Indian as well as international media and forced the government, in a landmark judgment in 1997, to enforce the fundamental rights of working women under Articles 14, 19, and 21 of the Constitution of India.

These guidelines later became the basis for a legislation in 2013 namely The Sexual Harassment of women at workplace (Prevention, prohibition and redressal) Act, enacted by the Indian Parliament to prevent the sexual harassment of women in the workplace.

According to this Act, "sexual harassment" includes any one or more of the following unwelcome acts or behaviors (whether directly or by implication), namely:

(i)   physical contact and advances; or

(ii) a demand or request for sexual favors; or

(iii) making sexually colored remarks; or

(iv) showing pornography; or

(v)   any other unwelcome physical, verbal, or non-verbal conduct of a sexual nature;

Under this Act, a workplace includes both organized and unorganized sectors. The workplace is a broad term including any and all government, private hospitals, sports institutions, administrations, and even households. As per section 2(a)(i) of the above said Act of 2013, this law protects every woman who is present at any given workplace, whether she works there or not. She might just be a usual visitor there.

According to Shawn Burn, a professor at California Polytechnic State University, sexual harassment works as a tool by insecure males to intimidate women to secure their position in the firm. More often than not, we have witnessed coworkers and seniors use dirty politics to ensure that they stay at the top by making the situation uncomfortable and negative for a thriving employee. These situations can lead to a traumatic effect on the targeted person and result in their downward spiraling performance.

Furthermore, traditionally, in a male-dominated world, women status have been normalized as sexual symbols. Women are not just objectified through movies but also by criteria for interview selection and designated roles. This generalization has made men habitually perceive women as objects, rather than an equally competent and capable individual working alongside.

In view of the reasons given above, 2019 saw a 5% increase in such sexual harassment cases, with 505 registered cases as per the National Crime Records Bureau. Whereas, in 2014, there were only 57 registered cases. One cannot ignore the fact that this data is partial, as 90% of the women work in the unorganized sector and have no means to lodge a complaint.

Following are the legal remedies that can be adhered to for taking action:

1. The apparent first step is to file a complaint with the ICC (Internal Complaint Committee). Any organization with more than 10 employees is mandated to form one. The final report given by the committee is also reflected in the annual report of the company.

2. This complaint can be filed within the first 3 months of the crime committed, and this time period of 3 months can be extended up to 6 based on the circumstances in which one was unable to report it.

3. The ICC primarily tries to reconcile the matter among the parties, but on its failure, the committee has to investigate within 90 days.

4. If the office environment makes you uncomfortable due to psychological distress from the aftermath, then you can request time off and even get yourself transferred under Section 12.

5. If the accused is proven guilty, their salary can be deducted by the ICC.

6. If you (the aggrieved party) are not satisfied, then you can file a suit in court under different sections of the Bharatiya Nyaya Sanhita 2023 (formerly known as the Indian Penal Code 1860) such as Section 296 penalizing obscene acts (quondam 294 of the IPC 1860), section 75 defining and penalizing sexual harassment (quondam 354 A of IPC 1860), and section 79 penalizing harming a woman's modesty (509 of IPC 1860).

7. There is a SHe-box online where you can file a complaint.

Several landmark judgments have significantly impacted the legal framework surrounding sexual harassment in the workplace in various jurisdictions. The Supreme Court of India, in the matter of Vishaka vs. the State of Rajasthan (1997), laid down the guidelines for dealing with sexual harassment in the workplace in the absence of legislation. The Vishaka judgement mandated employers to establish mechanisms to prevent and redress complaints of sexual harassment. The judgment also defined sexual harassment and directed employers to create a complaints committee, ensure a safe working environment, and take necessary measures for prevention. Further, in the case of Apparel Export Promotion Council vs. A.K. Chopra (1999), the court further reinforced the principles laid down in the Vishaka judgment. The Supreme Court held that physical contact was not essential to establish sexual harassment and emphasized the psychological impact on the victim.

Stalking

When most people think of stalking, they may imagine a stranger prowling around a person's house at night, showing up at their office uninvited, or following a person from place to place. However stalking involves much more than just following someone around. Often, the person stalking threatens or intends to harm the person they are stalking.

"On a chilly morning in November, when Sreepriya, 22, was halted on her way to college by Rohit Kumar, her stalker from a few months. He demanded she confess her love for him. When she denied his forceful request, Rohit gashed her cheek with a razor" may be considered an annotation for the inclusive and pervasive definition of stalking. Additionally, stalking can also occur online.

It is terrifying to be a victim of stalking. The person stalking you might be a random stranger, a casual acquaintance, or someone you used to be close with. They might send you unwanted notes, letters, or gifts, contact you incessantly even when you say you don't want to talk to them and try to approach you online or in person. Many stalkers will also try to gather information about you from friends or family or show up coincidentally at places you often go. All of these stalking tactics are frightening and I wish you never face these. The NCRB report for 2018-2020 shows a downfall in cases from 9438 to 8512, respectively. However, this reduction can easily be attributed to Covid related restrictions. According to Scroll (An independent digital news publication), in 2018, every 55 minutes, a report of stalking was registered.

Cyber Stalking

Stalking is gender-neutral but not linear. It is a known fact that women face this issue predominantly. According to data from sources, approximately 75% of female stalking victims report experiencing unwanted phone calls, and other related stalking behaviours. In 2017, only 4,242 cases were filed across India and Maharashtra had the highest number of complaints, 301. However, In 2021, a total of 9,285 cases of stalking, as reported by the National Crime Records Bureau (NCRB). Maharashtra had the highest number of these cases, with 2,131 reported incidents, followed by Telangana with 1,265 cases, and Andhra Pradesh with 1,185 cases. This might not even need data to substantiate it as the reader themselves may have experienced or heard in their own friend's circle of being stalked online.

In the times of millennials and Gen Z's, online stalking has become a very common occurrence. Everyone is doing it in some form, but it is projected as cool, and if not that, then at least passable. However, this can take an ugly turn for some. For instance, a 17-year-old class 11 male student was apprehended for allegedly stalking and blackmailing a woman on social media, wherein he had sent messages that contained abusive and obscene content with threats to morph her images if she did not extend sexual favors to him.

Bharatiya Nyaya Sanhita 2023 defines stalking under section **78 (quondam 354 D of the IPC 1860) as:**

Any man who—

(i) follows a woman and contacts, or attempts to contact such woman to foster personal interaction repeatedly despite a clear indication of disinterest by such woman; or

(ii) monitors the use by a woman of the internet, email, or any other form of electronic communication, commits the offense of stalking:

Provided that such conduct shall not amount to stalking if the man who pursued it proves that—

(i) it was pursued for the purpose of preventing or detecting crime, and the man accused of stalking had been entrusted with the responsibility of prevention and detection of crime by the State; or

(ii) it was pursued under any law or to comply with any condition or requirement imposed by any person under any law; or

(iii) in the particular circumstances, such conduct was reasonable and justified.

Stalking has been rampant in India and the sad credit goes to our cinema culture, which has glorified stalker behavior as heroic and persistent. Throughout the storyline from the '70s, movies have centered around a hero stalking and, with persuasion, getting the girl. This grim legacy has been followed to date with movies like Tere Naam and passably progressive movies like Raanjhanaa and Toilet: Ek Prem Katha. This validates men to pursue women incessantly without consent, not realizing that it is a punishable crime.

Bharatiya Nyaya Sanhita, 2023 under Section 78 (2) (Section 354 (D) of erstwhile IPC 1860), has defined the punishment for stalking as follows:

a. Whoever commits the offense of stalking shall be punished with the first conviction with imprisonment of either description for a term which may extend to 3 years and shall also be liable to a fine; and be

b. punished on a second or subsequent conviction, with imprisonment of either description for a term which may extend to 5 years, and shall also be liable to a fine.

Just like every other social issue related to disrespecting women, stalking is also a matter that is silenced for fear of social stigma. Victim shaming and blaming is a concept we all have been an unfortunate part of.

Continuing the Sreepriya's incidence above

> "Sreepriya's father, who was an auto driver, knew about Rohit Kumar, the stalker. He warned the fellow but never filed a complaint. Once the matter was out of hand and the unfortunate incident took place, he let his daughter report it to the police with lots of apprehension."

For my readers, on the other hand, if they are facing problems remotely similar to stalking, it is advisable to take some action, even including the following:

1. Firstly, one should be aware that stalking is a punishable offense in all states.

2. Secondly, report an F.I.R at your nearest police station. Police might know better how to tackle such situations better.

3. You can also reach out to the National Commission for Women (NCW). The commission itself will reach out to the police.

4. If the case is grave, there will be an inquiry committee that investigates the case, including proof and witnesses.

5. Since stalking is not limited to physical precincts, thanks to the internet and its reach, you can prima facie report the crime to the platform where it is taking place.

6. You can complain to the Cyber Cells, which are specifically formed for cybercrime victims.

7. If a stalker is sending over lewd and vulgar content, one can intimate the platform through which this material is being sent. Applications like Instagram and WhatsApp provide blocking and reporting options. These apps are legally obliged to comply with The Information Technology (Intermediary Guidelines and Digital Media Ethics Code) Rules, 2021, to provide a grievance redressal mechanism that heeds your complaints and reverts within 15 days.

Despite the legal provisions, the implementation of anti-stalking laws in India faces several challenges, including:

- **Awareness:** There is a lack of awareness among women about their legal rights and the recourse available to them.

- **Social Stigma:** Many victims hesitate to report stalking due to the social stigma associated with it.

- **Law Enforcement:** There are instances of inadequate response from law enforcement agencies, which can discourage victims from seeking help.

The government and various organizations continue to work on improving the implementation of anti-stalking laws through awareness campaigns, training of law enforcement personnel, and providing better support systems for victims. Understanding the legal framework and the challenges involved is crucial for effectively addressing the issue of stalking in India and ensuring the safety and dignity of women.

Voyeurism

The newspapers nowadays are filled with excerpts revealing the reality of the growing crime against women in India. Voyeurism is one such offense against women that sometimes lays the basis for other major offenses. According to the NCRB report of 2019, the cases recorded were 2419, whereas it was 1393 in 2018. In Maharashtra, the maximum number of cases was recorded, followed by Delhi. In India, the cases of voyeurism are rising every year. In the year 2020, 144 complaints of voyeurism were filed with the National Commission for Women.

Voyeurism is defined as a practice under which one gains sexual pleasure by secretly observing or watching others, either naked or engaged in any intimate or sexual activity like bathing, disrobing, etc., or engaging in any activity that would usually be considered 'private.' The victims of voyeurism are not aware that they are being watched, recorded, or photographed as they believe themselves to be in a situation of complete privacy. Another important factor is that they have not given any consent to such actions and so they are right in assuming this privacy.

Initially, the term voyeurism was limited only to physically peeping into homes, bathrooms, or other private places through windows, doors, or peepholes to gaze at the person engaged in some intimate activity. But with the advent of technology, voyeurism is now committed through the use of electronic devices, and electronic voyeurism has become the practice among the voyeurs. It has become easier and more convenient for the person to capture the intimate moments of the person without being physically present. The voyeuristic content is often used as "revenge porn" as these recordings or photos are leaked and used to blackmail the victim, which harasses the victim and their family mentally as well as physically.

If we look at the origin of laws related to voyeurism in India, a committee was set up under the chairmanship of former Chief Justice of India, J S Verma, which submitted its report on January 23, 2013, and the Criminal Law (Amendment) Act, 2013 was passed based on these recommendations that introduced voyeurism as an offense in India under Section 354C of the Indian Penal Code, 1860 along with other amendments in the act. The concept of voyeurism is based on the doctrine of reasonable expectation of privacy. Now, this law is present under the Bharatiya Nyaya Sanhita 2023 under section 77.

Under the doctrine of reasonable expectation of privacy, reasonable expectation of privacy refers to the circumstances in which a person has the

right to privacy or the right to be left alone. Thus, if a person expects privacy but it is intruded upon unlawfully, then the intruder can be held liable for this offence.

This doctrine was laid down in the case of the American Court in *Katz v. United States* (1967). The Court framed a two-prong test to ascertain whether this act can be considered private or not. The first test is whether the person has an actual (subjective) expectation of privacy in that space. Secondly, whether the person's expectation of privacy is (objectively) reasonable or not? If the answer to both questions is affirmative, then the person is considered to be in a private space, and the privacy of such a person could not be invaded. To clarify it further lets imagine that someone is doing something private in a public place, then the answer to question no-2 shall become non-afirmative and it will fail the test laid by doctrine of reasonable expectation of privacy.

In the case of *R v. Jarvis* (2019), this doctrine was applied in the case of voyeurism. In this case, the school teacher was charged with voyeurism as he was found guilty of recording photographs of the female student's breasts and upper bodies while they were engaged in ordinary school-related activities through the use of a camera pen.

The question that arose in this case was whether the circumstances were such that the victims expected privacy or not. The Court, in this case, laid down circumstances that need to be adhered to while determining the question of reasonable expectation of privacy, as follows:

- The location of the person when she is being recorded or observed.
- Whether the alleged conduct amounted to observation or recording.
- The consent of the victim for recording.
- How was the recording done?
- Content of the recording.
- Any rules, regulations, or policies that governed the observation or recording.
- Relationship between the person being recorded and the person who is recording.
- The purpose behind such recording or observing.
- Personal characteristics of the person who is being observed or recorded.

All these factors do not necessarily need to be present to consider the expectation of privacy. Moreover, in areas like washrooms, etc., the factors need not be implied as it is understood that a person expects privacy in such places. In this case, the teacher was held liable as privacy does not depend on confined walls but on the consideration of all circumstances and the consent of the person being recorded.

Voyeurism is explicitly mentioned as an offense under Section 77 of Bharatiya Nyaya Sanhita 2023. According to this Section, voyeurism is committed if someone watches or captures the image of a woman engaging in a private act in circumstances where she would usually have the expectation of not being observed either by the perpetrator or by any other person at the behest of the perpetrator, or disseminates such an image. In India, keeping the background and social situations in mind, the offense has not been made gender-neutral and can only be committed by a man against a woman. This Section is not against the principle of equality in the country as it comes under the umbrella of Article 15(3) of the Constitution of India and is a special provision for women.

For this Section, the term 'private act' is explained under Explanation 1 of the Section, which states that any act that is committed in areas usually considered private or under circumstances in which the victim's genitals, posterior, or breasts are exposed or covered only in underwear; or the victim is using the washroom or engaged in a sexual act. Essentially, all the acts that a person under normal circumstances will not engage in publicly can be categorised as "private act."

If anyone is found guilty and thus convicted under this Section, then:

- He is punishable with imprisonment of either description of a minimum of one year, which can extend up to 3 years, and is also liable for a fine if he is convicted for the first time.

- But in the case of a second or subsequent conviction, the person is liable for imprisonment of either description, which can range from 3 years to 7 years, and also for a fine.

Electronic voyeurism has been introduced in India under the Information Technology Act, 2000, by virtue of the IT Amendment Act, 2008, which came into force on 27 October 2009. The amendment was made because of the advancement in technology and how the use of smartphones and an internet connection can pose a grave threat to the modesty and integrity of women because they can be recorded through such covert means (hidden cameras, etc.) without them realizing it. The offender does not need to be in close proximity to the victim while committing the crime, and thus, sometimes, the offenders easily escape liability. The circulation of such obscene images worldwide with just a click can also prove to be fatal, and such incidents torment women.

According to Section 66E of the IT Act 2000, if any person voluntarily, i.e., intentionally or knowingly, captures, publishes, or transmits the image of private areas of any person without their consent, this act intrudes on the privacy of the victim, and the offender is liable for imprisonment which can extend to 3 years or a fine up to Rs. 2 lakh or both.

In a landmark judgement in the case of *State v. Shailesh (2019)*, Justice Susheel Bala Dagar held that voyeurism is a ridiculous type of enjoyment for men, whereas it causes mental trauma to women. Such acts infringe on the Right to Privacy of women, making them feel unsafe in places generally meant to be safe for women. In this case, the Supreme Court reiterated the judgment of *R. Rajagopal v. the State of Tamil Nadu* (1995) and stated that the Right to Privacy also includes the 'right of being left alone.'

In another case of *Rahul v. State* (2020), the appeal was filed by the accused, who was convicted by the trial court under Sections 376(2)(n), 354C, 506 of the Indian Penal Code, 1860 in the High Court. However, the High Court upheld the decision of the trial court, and the accused was convicted for the offense of rape and video graphing the act while clicking nude images of the victim.

Among the various measures which could be taken by government and NGO, the voyeurism should be tacked with the inclusion of Tech/AI and also through followings:

- Awareness campaigns.

- Prompt action against the offender.

- Cyber security

- Monitoring and surveillance of the area

- Community Policing

So by adopting a multi-faceted approach that includes legal, technological, social, and community-based measures, India can make significant progress towards addressing the voyeurism.

Word, Gesture, or Act Intended to Insult the Modesty of a Woman

The heading of the chapter is laden with heavy and long words with which many of us might be unfamiliar. However, one form of this crime namely eve-teasing, is a regular event on the roads and public places. According to statistics, 80-90% of girls in New Delhi have experienced eve-teasing. The term 'Eve-teasing,' often used to describe the harassment of women in public, originates from the Biblical figure Eve, symbolizing the idea of temptation. However, this term wrongly implies that women provoke such behaviour, trivializing the serious issue of sexual harassment. Unfortunately, in India, the term 'Eve-teasing' is often used to describe an insignificant offence of sexual harassment that insult a woman's dignity and are meant to demean her modesty. Perhaps the "good-natured" humour behind the name is the reason that only 1 out of 10,000 cases of eve-teasing are reported.

The IPC, now replaced with the Bharatiya Nyaya Sanhita 2023, has not mentioned any definition, but the term "modesty of women" is defined through her sexuality and any form of insult to disrespect the sexuality of a woman falls within the scope of this crime. Though a sensitive issue but it is not dealt very seriously, considering the rampant increase in the number of cases, as per the NCRB report. In 2019, 6937 cases were registered, and in 2021, the cases rose to 7788. The highest number of cases was registered in Andhra Pradesh.

Section 74 and 79 of the Bharatiya Nyaya Sanhita (quondam Section 354 and 509 respectively of the IPC 1860) respectively talk about "Assault or use of criminal force to woman with intent to outrage her modesty" and "Word, gesture or act intended to insult the modesty of a woman."

In 1995, an I.A.S officer, Rupan Deol Bajaj, was enjoying a party until Pal Singh, Inspector General of Police, decided to slap the posterior of the officer as a joke. Eventually and rightfully, in the turn of events, it became an infamous case of offense committed under section 509 of IPC.

The dignity and modesty of a woman are part of her identity. Any disrespect to it can harm the psychological balance of a woman. 98 percent of women have stated that sexual harassment on roads has affected their personal or academic development in one way or another.

It is absurd how lightly this can be taken sometimes and is often casually termed as "Gedi culture" in the Northern Parts of our country. The intensity of this crime is often undermined and taken lightly throughout the country. Insulting women based on their sexuality cannot be passed off as jocular banter, love, and courting, which is a popular mindset promoted by movies. The deeply layered reason is that women are considered inferior and feeble. Bullying them is an extension of misogyny, and it comes at no cost of the altercation, as women would rather ignore these remarks and move on. Almost every woman who steps out faces this issue.

But women need to answer back to these insults and know that this is a cognizable crime. If proven guilty, he will be punished for a minimum 1 year and can extend to 5 years (Sec. 74 of Bharatiya Nyaya Sanhita 2023) and may have to pay a fine. The offense here is non-compoundable, though it is bailable.

Section 74 of Bharatiya Nyaya Sanhita 2023 gives protection against assault or use of criminal force to a woman with intent to outrage her modesty.

Whoever assaults or uses criminal force to any woman, intending to outrage or knowing it to be likely that he will thereby outrage her modesty, shall be punished with imprisonment of either description for a term which shall not be less than one year but which may extend to 5 years, and shall also be liable to a fine.

It's important to note that these sections (74 and 79) are just a part of the laws in India aimed at protecting women from sexual harassment and assault and upholding their dignity and modesty.

Section 74 of Bharatiya Nyaya Sanhita 2023 pertains to the offense of **"Assault or criminal force** to woman with intent to outrage her modesty." This section is specifically designed to protect women from sexual harassment and addresses actions that are meant to insult the modesty or dignity of a woman.

Section 79 of Bharatiya Nyaya Sanhita 2023 (quondam 509 of the IPC 1860) pertains to the offense of "Word, gesture or act intended to insult the modesty of a woman." This section addresses the use of **words, gestures, or actions** that are intended to insult the modesty or dignity of a woman.

Here are some examples of situations that could be considered offenses under Bharatiya Nyaya Sanhita 2023 sections 74 and 79:

BNS Section 79

A man makes lewd comments to a woman in a public place, intending to insult her modesty. A person sends obscene messages to a woman through text or social media, intending to insult her modesty.

BNS Section 74

1. A man grabs a woman by her arm in a public place with the intention of outraging her modesty.

2. A man forcibly tries to kiss a woman in a public place with the intention of outraging her modesty.

3. A man touches a woman inappropriately on a crowded train with the intention of outraging her modesty.

It's important to note that in both sections, the accused must have intended to insult the modesty or dignity of the woman in question. The main difference between the 2 sections is that Section 74 specifically addresses physical actions, while Section 79 covers both physical actions and spoken words or gestures.

The lack of a proper redressal system for women is a reason why women are not confident in facing this issue head-on. The lack of fast-track courts merely delivers the message that the judicial system is not concerned about the safety of women. Moreover, the lack of support from the police, who tried to dismiss the complainant either by not registering the FIR with the excuse that it didn't take place in their jurisdiction or merely by taking an application to avoid making an official record.

While awareness campaign among women and appreciating their courage to file cases and make complaints shall always be helpful but I certainly believe that adoption of technology like AI could make a long strides towards protection of women against these verbal/gesture harassments.

Here are several ways AI can contribute to enhancing the safety and dignity of women:

- Implementing AI surveillance in public transportation to monitor and report incidents of harassment immediately.

- Facebook and Twitter use AI to detect and remove hate speech and harassment on their platforms.

- AI-powered mobile apps can provide women with safety features such as emergency contacts, real-time location sharing, and SOS alerts.
- AI-enabled public safety systems can detect and respond to verbal and physical harassment.

These technologies can analyse the user's environment and send alerts if they detect signs of distress. Recording offenses and gathering evidence through smart technology, combined with robust legal redressal mechanisms, can significantly contribute to creating safer environments for women.

Disrobing a Woman

Any person who sexually assaults or uses criminal force against any woman or abets such an act with the intention of disrobing or compelling her to be naked commits a crime that is punishable under Section 76 of the Bharatiya Nyaya Sanhita 2023. The **erstwhile Section 354 of the IPC 1860** mentioned such offence of use of any criminal force committed against a woman with the intention of outraging her modesty. The ambit of IPC 354 was widened by the introduction of Section 354 A and Section 354 B in 2013.

Now, Section 75 (1) of the Bharatiya Nyaya Sanhita 2023, deals with sexual harassment and punishment for sexual harassment, stating that a man committing any of the following acts:

I.   Physical contact and advances involving unwelcome and explicit sexual overtures; or

II. A demand or request for sexual favors; or

III. Showing pornography against the will of a woman; or

IV. Making sexually colored remarks.

Shall be guilty of the offense of sexual harassment and shall be punished as follows.

- Any man who commits the offense specified in clause (i), clause (ii), or clause (iii) above shall be punished with rigorous imprisonment for a term which may extend to 3 years, or with a fine, or with both.

- Any man who commits the offense specified in clause (iv) above shall be punished with imprisonment of either description for a term which may extend to one year, or with a fine, or with both.

This section clearly states that the act of sexual harassment caused by a person is punishable. Sexual harassment is not only an offense against an individual woman, but it is also a wrong against public morals and decent behavior.

Section 75 (1) is a cognizable and bailable offense, which can be tried by any magistrate.

Section 76 of the Bharatiya Nyaya Sanhita 2023 deals with assault or the use of criminal force against a woman with the intent to disrobe. *Any man who assaults or uses criminal force against any woman or abets such an act with the intention of disrobing or compelling her to be naked shall be punished with imprisonment of either description for a term not less than 3 years but which may extend to 7 years, and shall also be liable to a fine.*

This section clearly states that a man with intent to disrobe (undress) a woman using criminal force shall be liable for a prescribed term of punishment. Offenses under this section are also cognizable but non-bailable. Cases under this section can be tried by any magistrate.

Indecent behavior, not the age of the woman, is the criterion to determine the offense of outraging modesty punishable under Section 74 of the Bharatiya Nyaya Sanhita 2023. The word "modesty," as perceived under the section, refers to universally accepted womanly behavior or standard womanly notions and behavior.

However, what constitutes 'outraging the modesty of a woman' has not been defined under the Bharatiya Nyaya Sanhita, 2023. The courts determine whether the offense under this section has been committed or not based on the circumstances of the case. Such charges are very easy to make, and a man has little chance of rebuttal because an independent witness may not be available. But this situation acts, otherwise too, as, in general, these acts are more likely to occur in private spaces than public ones.

To really make sure that the accused is found guilty, one thing to be kept in mind is to maintain the line and sequence of events in the FIR and the trial. The inconsistency of events and the line of facts is a major reason behind many acquittals. At the same time, some incidents mentioned in the FIRs are so bizarre that a prudent person would not believe them. Also, nowadays it is often seen that women allege molestation even in cases where it is just an official quarrel and a matter of office discipline. Therefore, the courts have been ruling against the complainants and have been taking a very pragmatic view, determining each case based on the facts and circumstances surrounding it.

The only major thing that constitutes the essence of a woman's modesty is her sex. The wrong intention of the accused plays a major role in determining the crux of the offense. The courts explained that the act of pulling a woman and removing her saree, coupled with a request for sexual intercourse, is such as would outrage the modesty of a woman. Also, mere knowledge of the fact that the modesty is likely to be outraged is sufficient to constitute the offense and needs no further explanation of the intention of the offender.

For any complaints or redressal under section 74/75/76 of BNS 2023, one must keep in mind the following points.

1. The aggrieved person must be a woman.

2. All offenses related to sexual harassment, assault, etc., are cognizable criminal offenses. Police must take FIRs immediately.

3. Try to keep a witness, verbal recording, text records, etc.

4. An attempt with intention/knowledge is enough to file an FIR. Mere proof that the woman felt her modesty had been outraged would not satisfy the necessary ingredient of the offense.

5. Offenses except under section 354A (Sexual harassment) are non-bailable, and so arrest should happen; however, depending upon the gravity of the case, there could be police bail (75(1)) or regular bail (74 and 76).

6. File the FIR with the police without any fear of repercussion.

It is suggested not to confuse sexual harassment/assault with any disciplinary action at the office or over-reading a colleague of your company. You must be clear on the knowledge, intention, and action of the accused. What may be modest for one woman may not be for another. The man having knowledge that his act will outrage the modesty of the victim woman is the crux.

In the recent case of Manipur violence in 2023, which involved the disrobing and parading of women, the charges would typically attract this section. Two women from the Kuki-Zo community were disrobed, paraded naked, and gang-raped by a mob in the Thoubal district of Manipur. Hon. Hight court/Supreme court and our media all condemned the incidence and the SIT has been set up and the matter is sub judice. We definitely expect a strong judgement and guidelines from our legislators and judiciary.

Human Trafficking

In the movie "Gangubai kathiawadi" Ganga was enchanted by the spell of love by Ramanik. Despite having a loving family, she decided to run away from home with him in pursuit of a career in movies and a happy love life. How that played out for her is known to everyone, even to those who haven't seen the movie. It's also not uncommon to see Indian families raising their daughters as naive to maintain their innocence. However, they may not realize that this can unintentionally make their daughters, more vulnerable to manipulation or exploitation and luring. Many girls are lured by men through phone calls in the name of love and a promise of marriage, and then trafficked for either prostitution, slavery, or marriage.

Human trafficking is defined as the trade of humans for the purpose of forced labor, sexual slavery, or commercial sexual exploitation for the trafficker or others. This may encompass providing a spouse in the context of forced marriage, or the extraction of organs or tissues, including for surrogacy and ova removal. Human trafficking is a serious problem worldwide and is a violation of human rights. It involves the recruitment, transportation, transfer, harboring, or receipt of persons by means of threat, use of force, or other forms of coercion, deception, or abuse of power for the purpose of exploitation. Exploitation can include forced labor, sexual exploitation, and organ removal, among others.

Victims of human trafficking in India come from all regions and backgrounds, but the most vulnerable populations include women and children from poor and marginalized communities. Poverty, lack of education, and lack of job opportunities can make individuals more susceptible to trafficking. In many cases, victims are promised job opportunities or a better life, only to be subjected to exploitation and abuse once they reach their destination. The Indian government has taken steps to address human trafficking, including the enactment of the Immoral Traffic (Prevention) Act and the creation of anti-trafficking units within the police force.

In 2021, 6,533 people were trafficked, of which 3,656 were adults. Nepal and Bangladesh are the 2 countries from which the most trafficked people are brought to India. In terms of Indian states, Maharashtra has the highest number of cases. It is alarming that the cases are only on the rise instead of declining despite safety precautions and traceable locations.

In India, trafficking is addressed under several provisions of the Bharatiya Nyaya Sanhita 2023 as well as specific legislation mentioned below:

- Section 143 of the BNS (quondam Section 370 of the IPC 1860): This section pertains to the offense of trafficking, stating that whoever recruits, transports, transfers, harbors, or receives a person(s) through the use of force or threat, or by means of coercion, deception, or abuse of power, with the intention of exploiting them, shall be punished.

- Section 145 of BNS 2023 (quondam Section 371 of the Indian Penal Code 1860): This section deals with the offense of habitually importing, exporting, removing, buying, selling, trafficking, or dealing in slaves.

- The Immoral Traffic (Prevention) Act, 1956: This act provides for the prevention of trafficking in persons for the purpose of prostitution and punishes those who buy or sell a person for the purpose of prostitution.

- The Protection of Children from Sexual Offenses (POCSO) Act, 2012: This act provides for the protection of children from sexual abuse and exploitation and includes provisions that criminalize trafficking of children for sexual purposes.

It's important to note that these laws and provisions are just a part of the legal framework aimed at addressing human trafficking in India, and the specific provisions applied in a given case can depend on the circumstances and nature of the trafficking offense. Additionally, while these laws provide a framework for addressing trafficking, it's crucial to ensure they are effectively enforced and the victims receive the support and services they need to recover from their horrific experiences. The Bharatiya Nyaya Sanhita 2023 has the following set of punishments to deter this crime:

- The offender who has taken the victim for exploitation under section 143 (quondam Section 370 of IPC 1860) will be jailed for not less than 7 years, which can extend to a lifetime, and/or a fine.

- If the offender has sexually exploited a victim, they will be jailed for 3 years under section 144 of BNS 2023 (quondam Section 370 of IPC 1860).

- If a person is found guilty of dealing in slavery, they will be sent to jail for up to 10 years, as per section 145 (quondam Section 371 of IPC 1860).

- Sections 95 to 99 of the Bharatiya Nyaya Sanhita (BNS) specifically address trafficking offenses against children and impose stringent punishments on offenders.

Legal Protection against Trafficking:

- Article 23 of the Constitution of India states that forced labor, including begging and human trafficking, is strictly prohibited.

- Under section 141 & 144 of BNS 2023, anyone who traffics a girl under the age of 21 for sexual activity or other explotations with a third person will be sent to jail for up to 10 years and may also be liable for a fine.

- Section 146 (374 of IPC 1860) deals with forced labor, and the offender will be jailed for a year and might also be fined.

As members of society, knowing the laws is not enough. It is important to help these victims in normalizing their lives. Be alert in noticing and informing the police if you suspect trafficking activities. Secondly, victims should not be treated differently or with excessive pity. Help them reintegrate into society.

The government introduced the Ujjawala Scheme in 2016 for for Prevention of Trafficking and Rescue, Rehabilitation and Re-Integration of Victims of Trafficking for Commercial Sexual Exploitation, which rescues and rehabilitates victims. The rehabilitation centers or shelters being formed and constructed by the police, NGO and other governmental bodies through the funding under this scheme, which helps women who are deserted, to get reintegrated with the society.

With the increase in technology and its use by perpetrators, it has become easier for them to find their prey among innocent and naive girls. They target girls who are either economically disadvantaged or not educated enough. It is not easy to safeguard them, especially in the world of Facebook and Instagram. While it may be challenging to monitor every action online and offline, we can support victims by helping them report incidents to the police and assisting in their reintegration into society.

Acid Attack

An acid attack, also called acid throwing, vitriol attack, or vitriolage, is a form of violent assault involving the act of throwing acid or a similarly damaging substance onto the body of another, with the intention to hurt, disfigure, or seek revenge and coerce the victim to do or abstain from doing something. The perpetrators of these attacks throw corrosive liquids at their victims, usually targeting their faces, burning them, and damaging skin tone and color, often without intending to kill the person. Acid attacks can lead to permanent, partial, or complete blindness, among other serious physical, psychological, and social consequences.

Acid attacks often occur as revenge against a woman who rejects a proposal of marriage or a sexual advance. Societal situations, poverty, gender bias, and women's positions in particular societies or nations, as compared to men, play significant roles in these types of attacks. Generally, these cases are more prevalent in underdeveloped and  developing countries. According to the Acid Survivors Trust International, globally, 15,000 cases occur annually, with 80% of the victims being women, making it a gender-based crime. The National Crimes Record Bureau reported 202 recognized cases of acid attacks in India in 2023 (240 in 2019 Acid 182 in 2020). However, the actual number of cases is likely over 1,000, as many go unreported due to fear and societal pressure.

India has the highest number of acid attacks globally each year (ranging from 250 to 300), and despite actions taken by the Indian Government and the Supreme Court of India, the crime is on the rise. This increase can be attributed to the patriarchal ideology prevalent in India and the country's inadequate legal system, which does not deliver efficient and timely remedies to the victims.

The criminal laws of India were amended to address this crime, and sections 326A and 326B were added to the Indian Penal Code in 2013 to create a special provision. Section 326A of the IPC criminalizes throwing, administering, or attempting to throw acid on any person, irrespective of gender, with the intent to disfigure or maim that person, causing permanent or partial damage. The newly incorporated Bharatiya Nyaya Sanhita offers this provision under Section 124(1) and 124(2). In contrast to a common understanding, for a person to be convicted under this offense, it is not required that the actual damage should occur or disfigurement must be irreversible in nature. This offense is cognizable and non-bailable. FIRs must be registered by the police, and arrests should be made immediately.

Under Section 124(1) of the Bharatiya Nyaya Sanhita 2023, the punishment for administering an acid attack is a minimum of 10 years, which may extend to life imprisonment at the court's discretion. The punishment for attempting to throw acid on a person is 5-7 years under Section 124 of Bharatiya Nyaya Sanhita 2023, irrespective of the nature of the damage caused to the victim. The victim is entitled to compensation, and the fine must cover the victim's medical expenses. The compensation should be payable in addition to the payment of the fine by the culprit.

The heinous crime of acid attacks is addressed not only by the Bharatiya Nyaya Sanhita and Bharatiya Sakshya Adhiniyam, 2023 but also includes relevant provisions in the Bharatiya Nagrik Suraksha Sanhita 2023. These provisions are contained in Section 396 of the

Bharatiya Nagrik Suraksha Sanhita 2023 (quondam Section 357A of the Code of Criminal Procedure). Further, Subsection 396(7) of the Bharatiya Nagrik Suraksha Sanhita 2023 (quondam Section 357B of the CrPC) clarifies that the compensation mentioned in the predecessor section will be provided in addition to the compensation already provided under Section 65, Section 70, and Subsection (1) of Section 124 of the Bharatiya Nyaya Sanhita, 2023 (quondam Section 376A to 376E of IPC 1860). The CrPC mandates that all hospitals, regardless of their nature (local, public, private), provide the victim with immediate emergency first aid free of cost.

The following quick facts should be helpful for any complaint and redressal thereof:

1. Acid attack is a cognizable criminal offense and is non-bailable. Police must make arrests immediately.

2. A mere attempt is enough to file an FIR. Actual damage need not be proved.

3. Acid should not be sold to anyone under the age of majority, i.e., 18 years.

4. Acid attack remains a crime even against a legally married wife who has an extramarital affair.

5. Every hospital is legally obligated to provide free first aid treatment.

6. The penalty is always in addition to compensation when the accused is convicted.

7. The first action after an acid attack is to douse the affected area with plenty of water, protect the eyes, and move immediately to a hospital. Do not rub the affected area with your hands, clothes, or other materials.

8. File the FIR with the police as soon as possible without any fear of retribution.

One can understand the social stigma, but when this happens to anybody, one should go all out, starting from rural complaint platform (like gram panchayat) to social/digital media, to make sure that police and administration do not act even slightly lenient in prosecuting and punishing the offender. Even though "looking at inner beauty and not physical appearance" may sound rubbish, have hope that our society has good people as well, and believe in your medical fraternity to heal you to live a normal and happy life ahead.

In the matter of Laxmi vs. Union Of India and Ors. [2014 SCC (4) 427], wherein Laxmi, an acid attack survivor, filed a Public Interest Litigation (PIL) seeking stringent regulations on the sale of acid and compensation for acid attack victims. The case led to a landmark judgment addressing the issues of regulation of sale of acid, the compensation and rehabilitation of victim. The supreme court directed all states and Union Territories to frame rules to regulate the sale of acid and it could only be sold to individuals above 18 years, and sellers were required to maintain a register recording the details of the buyer, including the purpose of purchase and also report stocks and transactions to the local police. The compensation was defined to include cost of treatment and rehabilitation too. Also the Private hospitals were directed to provide free treatment to acid attack victims, including reconstructive surgery. The Court also appointed the National Legal Services Authority (NALSA) to monitor the adherence of the directives. However, unfortunately, the reporting (around 60% goes unreported) and the conviction rates for acid attack cases have been low. In 2021, only 2.46% of cases were disposed of in courts, reflecting the slow judicial process and many other Implementation Gaps.

Attempt to Commit Rape

As Buddha said, karma does not begin when you take the action; it starts manifesting when you think about the action. In line with this philosophical thought, it is necessary to state that a crime that is unfinished is still a crime because it was carried out with the intention of fulfillment.

There are 3 stages in which rape is committed:

1. Intention to commit

2. Preparation for it

3. Attempt to commit

The Hon. High Court, in the landmark judgment of Madan Lal vs. State Of J&K on 6 August 1997, revered the judgment of the Trial Court in conviction of Madan Lal, a headmaster who attempted to rape a student. He was booked under Section 376, read with Section 511 of the Indian Penal Code.

The Supreme Court has held that an attempt to commit an offense is an act or series of acts, which leads inevitably to the commission of the offense, unless something unless something unforeseen or unintended by the doer occurs to prevent it. An attempt may be described as an act done in part-execution of a criminal design, amounting to more than mere preparation but falling short of actual consummation and possession. It includes all the elements of the substantive crime except the final act of consummation due to some obstacle. In other words, an attempt consists of the intent to commit a crime falling short of its actual commission.

The difference between preparation and an attempt to commit an offense consists chiefly in the greater degree of determination, and what is necessary to prove that an offense of an attempt to commit rape has been committed is that, the accused has gone beyond the stage of preparation. If an accused strips a girl naked and then, making her lie down, and then engages in inappropriate sexual contacts, ejaculates himself, then it is difficult to say that it was a case of mere assault under Section 74 of the Bharatiya Nyaya Sanhita 2023 (Quondam 354 IPC 1860) and not an attempt to commit rape under Section 63 read with 62 of the BNS 2023 (Quondam Section 376 read with Section 511 IPC).

If the facts and circumstances of the case suggest that rape, as defined under BNS as far as insertion goes, could not be completed just due to a reason which was not really in the control and disposal of the accused, then the offense of an attempt to commit rape is clearly established, and conviction under 63 read with 62 of the BNS 2023 is an appropriate outcome.

Whoever attempts to commit an offense punishable by this Code with imprisonment for life or imprisonment, or to cause such an offense to be committed, and in such attempt does any act toward the commission of the offense, shall, where no express provision is made by this Code for the punishment of such an attempt, be punished with imprisonment of any description provided for the offense, for a term which may extend to one-half of the imprisonment for life or, as the case may be, one-half of the longest term of imprisonment provided for that offense, or with such fine as is provided for the offense, or with both. As Section 62 of the BNS 2023 deals with the offense of "attempt to commit offenses punishable with imprisonment for life or other imprisonments." In the case of attempted rape, this section can be applied to prosecute individuals who have attempted to commit the crime of rape but have not been successful in doing so.

Actually, the offense of attempt to rape can be attracted even if the accused has not undressed, as the attempt to commit an offense begins when the accused commences to do an act with the necessary intention, and it passes beyond just preparation.

If you witness an attempted rape or suspect that someone is in immediate danger of being sexually assaulted, it's important to take immediate action to help the victim and stop the perpetrator. Here are some steps you can take:

- Call emergency services: Dial the local emergency number, such as 100 or the women's helpline at 1091 or another relevant number, to report the incident and request assistance. Give the operator as much information as possible, including the location, description of the victim and the perpetrator, and any other relevant details.

- Offer assistance to the victim: If it's safe to do so, approach the victim and offer to help. Ask if they are okay and if they need medical attention. Reassure them that they are not to blame for what happened and that you are there to help.

- Confront the perpetrator: If possible, try to confront the perpetrator and demand that they stop what they are doing. If they are armed or dangerous, do not engage them and wait for the police to arrive.

- Gather evidence: If you can, try to gather evidence such as photos, videos, or eyewitness accounts that can help law enforcement in their investigation.

- Provide support to the victim: After the incident, it's important to continue to provide support to the victim. Offer to accompany them to the hospital or to the police station to make a report. Let them know that they can reach out to you for support and that you are there for them.

- At last, show the courage to be the witness in legal proceedings. You may have your own situation, but this is one of the fundamental duties our constitution bestows on us.

In a landmark Judgment in case of Aman Kumar & Anr. vs State Of Haryana (AIR 2004 SC 1497) the Hon. Supreme Court, after examining the evidence and legal provisions, upheld the charges and conviction.

The Court elucidated that to constitute an attempt, the accused must have committed an act towards the commission of the crime that is more than merely preparatory. The act must be proximate to the intended crime. The Court noted that in the present case, the appellants had caught hold of the victim and made attempts to undress her, which clearly demonstrated their intention to commit the offense of rape. The appellants' actions had crossed the stage of preparation and had entered the stage of an attempt to commit the offense.

The judgment emphasized the legal distinction between mere preparation and an attempt, where an attempt involves direct movement towards the commission of the crime after preparations have been made. It provides guidance on how courts should interpret and apply the provisions related to attempts to commit crimes, particularly in the context of sexual offenses.

Remember, victim's safety should be the top priority under all circumstances. Attempt to rape is one of most serious crime, and it's important to report directly or help the victim to report it to the authorities so that they can take the necessary action to bring the perpetrator to justice.

Through loud reading of headlines, increasing the volume when the news is on, or the exact opposite; in a hushed voice; every girl growing up is discreetly made aware of the crime "rape." It would be a moot point to give an introduction to rape here. Repeated echoing of words like "victim," "patriarchal society," "old laws," "injustice," and "victim blaming" can be heard associated with rape. One has to be living under a rock to be unaware of this, but the word rape can still send chills down a woman's or even a responsible citizen's spine. None of us can hide our disgust at uttering the word "rape" without reeling back in our minds, which takes us to an inhuman case that we read about. The Hindi word "balatkar" means to use force, and the word "rape" has been taken from the Latin word "rapio," which means to seize. Sociologically, these terms came into being when the crime was not against women but against the property of men.

Under the British Raj, when the IPC was first drafted in 1860, What is jarring is that married women could not claim to have been raped by their husbands, as they were legal holdings in the hands of their lawfully wedded husbands. This was the patriarchal representation of the English system and since then, Indian society has carried the burden of this mindset. The word itself is problematic, depriving women of their individuality, self-respect, and social status. Insensitivity is not limited to the word only but can also be seen, as to how, these crimes are handled by authorities and in the aftermath of these crimes in our society.

In the 21st century, one must notice that rape is a crime against a woman, not an attack on her integrity, social position, or a way to take revenge on the family they belong to. A common theme seen in the movies of the 70s was of a hero, not a protagonist, avenging the rape of his sister by killing the rapists. This way, he was restoring his sister's "izzat (respect and honor)". The crime was never against the heroine since she was to be kept pristine. In Movie Ramleela (2013), the sister-in-law was chased down the temple to be robbed of her modesty as a way to get back at family rivals. This situation highlights themes of honor, revenge, and the use of women as pawns in family feuds.

The intent for this crime might be different depending on how they want to use a woman; their animalistic tendencies remain the same if not more. This crime, in Sec 63 of BNS 2023 (quondam Section375 of IPC 1860), is defined as:

Rape—A man is said to commit "rape" if he—

(a) penetrates his penis, to any extent, into the vagina, mouth, urethra, or anus of a woman, or makes her do so with him or any other person; or

(b) Inserts, to any extent, any object or a part of the body, not being the penis, into the vagina, the urethra, or anus of a woman, or makes her do so with him or any other person; or

(c) Manipulates any part of the body of a woman so as to cause penetration into the vagina, urethra, anus, or any part of the body of such woman, or makes her do so with him or any other person; or

(d) Applies his mouth to the vagina, anus, or urethra of a woman, or makes her do so with him or any other person, under the circumstances falling under any of the following 7 descriptions:—

- **First**—Against her will.

- **Secondly**—Without her consent.

- **Thirdly**—With her consent, when her consent has been obtained by putting her or any person in whom she is interested in fear of death or hurt.

- o **Fourthly** —With her consent, when the man knows that he is not her husband and that her consent is given because she believes that he is another man to whom she is, or believes herself to be, lawfully married.

- o **Fifthly** —With her consent when, at the time of giving such consent, by reason of unsoundness of mind, intoxication, or the administration by him personally or through another of any stupefying or unwholesome substance, she is unable to understand the nature and consequences of that to which she gives consent.

- o **Sixthly** —With or without her consent, when she is under 18 years of age.

- o **Seventhly** —When she is unable to communicate consent.

The trauma of this atrocity, despite being grave, is shared by 64.5 women per lakh. This has seen a significant increase since 2020, where the crime rate per lakh women was 56.5. The punishment for the convicted, as per BNS 2023, is divided into different sections based on the nature of the rape:

1. Section 64 (1) of BNS 2023 (Quondam 376 of IPC 1860) mentions that the punishment will be for ten years, which can extend to life imprisonment, along with a fine.

2. As per Section 66 of BNS 2023 (Quondam 376A of IPC 1860), if the victim goes into a vegetative state (The case of Aruna Shanbaug), the punishment can be anywhere from 20 years to a life sentence.

3. Section 67 of BNS 2023 (Quondam 376B of IPC 1860) says that if a man, during his separation from his wife, rapes her, he will be sentenced to 2 years up to 7 years and a fine.

4. According to Section 68 of BNS 2023 (Quondam 376C of IPC 1860), if the rape is committed by an authority, they will be imprisoned for 5 to 10 years and fined.

5. The law also recognizes the cruelty of crimes committed by a group, and hence the punishment for gang rape as per 70(1) (Quondam 376D of IPC 1860) ranges from 20 years to life imprisonment and a fine.

6. For repeat offenders, as per Section 71 (Quondam 376E of BNS 2023), it is life imprisonment or the death penalty.

7. Under Section 72 (Quondam 228A of IPC 1860), if anyone publishes/prints the identity of the victim and makes it public, they will be jailed for a maximum of 2 years and fined.

Even with such severe punishments, crime is not subsiding and, in fact, increasing each year. If we talk about reported cases of rape (which is far less than the actual number of cases) in 2021, it is 31,677 compared to 28,046 in 2020. The conviction rate in India in 2021 was 24.8.

Rape is a serious and widespread problem that affects individuals across the world. According to the World Health Organization (WHO), 1 in 3 women globally experience physical or sexual violence in their lifetime, and this number is likely an underestimate due to under-reporting. The problem of rape is compounded by a lack of adequate legal protections and support for survivors, as well as a culture of victim blaming and discrimination. This can make it difficult for victims to come forward and get the help they need, and it can also make it difficult for law enforcement to prosecute perpetrators.

In the matter of *Ramkripal S/O Shyamlal Charmakar v. State of Madhya Pradesh (2007)* wherein the validity and strength of circumstantial evidence was questioned and The Supreme Court, after carefully examining the evidence on record, came to the conclusions that the circumstantial evidence was strong and pointed directly towards the guilt of the accused. The evidence included the recovery of the victim's body and the medical evidence indicating sexual assault and strangulation and Considering the brutality of the crime and the circumstances of the case, the Court upheld the death sentence awarded by the Trial Court and confirmed by the High Court.

As the opinions and facts given above indicate, rape is not a isolated crime; it is heavily influenced by our point of view toward women and their values. Unless there is a shift in this thought process, the crime will always be on the rise. Teaching boys about boundaries and guiding girls on safety measures are the first steps toward stabilizing the crime, and for it to decline, a lot in our social system needs to change.

There have been efforts in recent years to raise awareness about the issue of rape and to improve support for survivors. This includes increasing funding for services such as crisis hotlines, rape crisis centers, and legal assistance, as well as implementing laws and policies to better protect survivors and bring perpetrators to justice. However, much more needs to be done on a global scale to address the problem of this heinous crime. This includes changing and adjusting the cultural and religious thought and beliefs that contribute to such violence against women, as well as providing better education to children, use of technologies and other resources to prevent rape and support survivors. I personally think that, we as responsible society members should help and do our best towards rehabilitation of rape victims by accepting them as our celebrity, daughter in laws and preferred employees both in government sector and private sector. Rather than feeling pity about them, we should help them to be in position that they are full of resources and capacity to bring change in society.

SECTION 2

CHILDREN

Introduction – protection under **Bharatiya Nyaya Sanhita,** 2023 erstwhile Indian Penal Code, 1860., Juvenile Justice Act, 2015., Information Technology Act, 2000., Protection of Child from Sexual Offenses Act, 2012.

The phrase "the child is the father of the man" is a line from the great poet William Wordsworth. The full verse reads:

"The Child is father of the Man;

And I could wish my days to be Bound each to each by natural piety."

The phrase means that the personality and character of a person are formed in childhood and that our experiences and events during childhood shape who we become as adults. The phrase highlights the importance of childhood experiences and the role they play in shaping our lives and personalities and, finally, a society and nation. A healthy childhood is the origin of healthy and happy mankind on the planet.

In our country, Children's Day is celebrated on November 14 every year to increase awareness of the rights, care, and education of children. It serves as a reminder that we should cherish and nurture our children, as they will go on to become the adults of the future. It is important to note that the newly enacted Bharatiya Nyaya Sanhita (BNS) 2023 includes a general provision exempting all children below the age of seven from any criminal liability. This exemption underscores the legal principle that children under this age lack the maturity to understand the consequences of their actions, and therefore cannot be held criminally responsible. This provision aligns with established principles of juvenile justice, reinforcing the protection of young children within the legal framework. Sections 93 to 99 of the Bharatiya Nyaya Sanhita (BNS) 2023 cover various offenses related to children, including abandonment, exploitation, and abuse. These sections introduce provisions that strengthen legal protections for children and impose strict penalties on those who violate these protections

This section is dedicated to those calm, cute, peaceful, and lovely children who are considered sacred and godly.

Children and the Indian Legal System

Children are future assets and the most valuable for any country, but at the same time, they are the most vulnerable. A child's quality of life depends on many internal factors like gender, color, heredity and, at the same time, many external factors like social environment, physical, mental, economic, psychological status, drug abuse, etc. The brain functions and develops during childhood, primarily functioning based on the emotional quotient rather than logic (at least until the age of 18), and this ongoing brain development is influenced by all the above-mentioned external factors. So for a child to lead a quality life and become a responsible member of this planet, we need to give them a fair environment to live and grow.

This basic objective of giving every child a fair chance to live originates from the need of binding our society, states, and nations with a common minimum requirement/law to treat a child irrespective of race, caste, creed, sex, color, and nationality. The United Nations Convention on the Rights of the Child (UNCRC) is a legally binding agreement for all United Nations countries and sets out the basic civil, cultural, and social rights for a child. This is the most widely accepted law on the protection of children and makes the foundation of any new legislation that is brought into effect in any country. This treaty treats children not as charity recipients but as a privileged class of the population based on their stage of development and age. As per the basic definition of UNCRC, a child is any human being below the age of 18 years. UNCRC gives 4 fundamental rights to every child: survival, protection, development, and participation.

India's children continue to face some of the harshest conditions anywhere in the world, with high malnutrition, child labor and forced begging, sexual offenses, and childhood illnesses such as diarrheal disease. Due to the inherent innocence and immaturity, which are usually directly related to a child's age, they make an offender's favorite victim. In India, too, a child has been defined to mean a human being of age starting from 0 to 18 years.

Article 15 of the Constitution of India gives power to the State to make special provisions for children. On the other hand, Articles 39(e) and (f), 45, and 47 further make the State responsible for ensuring that all needs of children are met and their basic human rights are protected. Entry 5 of the Concurrent List (Schedule VII) of the Constitution of India provides for the fields on which the Parliament or State Legislatures can legislate on the children.

Also, the National Policy for Children 2013 affirms the central and state government commitment to treat every single child in the country as unique and supremely important national asset. In line with the 4 fundamental rights of UNCRC, survival, health, nutrition, development, education, protection, and participation are the undeniable rights of every child and are the key priorities of this policy.

Children in India are protected by many legislations like Bharatiya Nyaya Sanhita 2023, the Juvenile Justice Act, and the Information Technology Act, etc., but the fair implementation of these laws remains a challenge. In view of this, I decided to have a separate section dedicated to our beloved children and the future of our nation.

The basic aim here is to highlight the rights of children and the various types of child abuse that are committed in India and abroad. An innocent child often bears the burden of suffering in silence. It's our collective responsibility to recognize these hidden struggles and offer support. By fostering a culture of empathy, awareness, and active intervention, we can ensure that no child has to endure their pain alone. Every small act of kindness and vigilance can make a world of difference in the life of a child who needs it most. The topics shall give critical insights into the abuses of children that are being committed on a daily basis.

Before 1839, there used to be the concept of authority and control, and it was an accepted norm that the father of children had absolute rights over them.

It was in the late twenties that the rights of children started to emerge.

As child rights are the main pillars on which the offenses are further classified and, in time to come, some other offenses may be codified, I want to focus on the various rights our children have, and any violation of those rights is very much an offense irrespective of their codification under one or other legislation. So even if there is no mention of an offense against children in any of the Acts/legislation/rules/regulation or guidelines etc., those are triable offenses if those actions of a person violate children's rights. Our children have the following rights at a macro level for which one or other Act, policy, guidelines or charter shall have recourse:

1. Right of survival—health, nutrition, medication, and home care

2. Right to have a family environment, love, and trustworthy people around

3. Right to have parental care and fair treatment from parents

4. Right to education, play, and recreation

5. Right to be protected against sexual abuse and exploitation

6. Right against any commercial/economic exploitation

7. Right to the preferable administration and implementation of the above rights

Offenses like neglect, cruelty, underage employment, sexual exploitation, child intoxication, child kidnapping, bullying, trafficking, etc., are all violations of one or more of the above basic rights of a child. That's why, while I will list the offenses and talk about the recourse against those offenses in the last chapter of this section, I am basing my remaining chapters on the further detailing of these rights.

Right of Survival - Health, Nutrition, Medication, and Home Care

The right to survival is a fundamental and universal right of children, recognized by international law. This right encompasses the right to life, the right to health, and the right to adequate nutrition.

Survival is the most basic and most important right for a child, and this includes:

- Provision of an identity

- Access to healthcare and medical services in emergency situations

- Prevention of disease/pandemics through the existing healthcare network

- Access to shelter/home/foster home

- Access to nutritional facilities for children in need of care and protection

The United Nations Convention on the Rights of the Child (UNCRC), in Articles 7, 24, and 27, provides for the right of a child to access adequate healthcare and standard of living. Article 7 of the convention specifies that every child shall be registered immediately after birth and shall have the right from birth to a name, the right to acquire a nationality, and, as far as possible, the right to know and be cared for by his or her parents.

Article 24 of the convention commits national governments to diminish infant and child mortality, ensure the provision of necessary medical assistance and healthcare to all children with an emphasis on the development of primary healthcare, combat disease and malnutrition, and ensure appropriate prenatal and postnatal healthcare for mothers. Article 27 of the convention emphasizes recognizing the rights of every child to a standard of living adequate for the child's physical, mental, spiritual, moral, and social development.

The United Nations General Assembly adopted universal declaration of human right and Article 25, states that everyone has the right to a standard of living that is adequate for the health and well-being of themselves and their family, including food, clothing, shelter, housing, and other elements. Article 25 lays special emphasis on motherhood and childhood. Again, in the ICESCR (International Covenant on Economic, Social and Cultural Rights), which came into force in 1976, Article 11 states that the state parties recognize the right of everyone to an adequate standard of living for themselves and their family, including adequate food, clothing, and housing.

The right to life means that children have the right to live and grow up in a safe and secure environment, free from violence, abuse, and exploitation. Governments have a responsibility to protect children from harm and to ensure that their lives are not threatened by poverty, conflict, or other factors.

The right to health means that children have the right to access quality healthcare services, including preventive and curative care. This includes access to safe water, sanitation, and adequate nutrition, as well as immunization and other essential health services.

The right to adequate nutrition means that children have the right to adequate food and to be free from hunger. This includes access to nutritious foods, such as fruits and vegetables, as well as adequate quantities of food to meet their hunger and nutritional needs.

In practice, the right to survival of children is often violated, particularly in low- and middle-income countries. However, governments, international organizations, and civil society groups are working together to promote and protect this right through measures such as improving access to healthcare and nutrition, promoting good health practices, and addressing poverty and inequality.

In India, the right to survival of children is recognized by the Constitution and several laws and policies. Despite this, the survival of many children in India remains at risk due to poverty, malnutrition, lack of access to healthcare, and other factors. India has one of highest infant mortality rate, with an estimated 34 infant deaths per 1,000 live births in 2019. Malnutrition remains a major problem in India among children under the age of 5 years, with over 36% underweight, 38% of stunted, and 21% being wasted,

Child survival and development hinge on basic needs to support life. Among these, a safe, healthy, and clean environment is fundamental. Children are exposed to serious health risks from environmental hazards. Environmental risk factors often act in concert, and their effects are exacerbated by adverse social and economic conditions, such as poverty, and malnutrition.

The Indian government has implemented several initiatives to promote and protect the right to survival of children in the country, including the Integrated Child Development Services (ICDS) program, which provides health and nutrition services to children and pregnant/ lactating women. The government has also launched the National Health Mission, which aims to provide universal access to healthcare services.

The infant mortality rate in India in 2023-24 is expected to be 25.8/1000 and which is a very good improvement compared to earlier years but many children in India still face challenges to their survival. Malnutrition remains a major problem, with over 50% of children under the age of 5 being undernourished. In addition, access to healthcare remains limited in many rural areas, and child labor and child abuse remain prevalent.

Civil society organizations and non-governmental organizations are also working to promote and protect the right to survival of children in India with the scheme like mid-day meals in elementary schools. These groups work to raise awareness about child rights, provide health and nutrition services, and advocate for better policies and practices to protect children.

In conclusion, while the right to survival of children is recognized in India, much more needs to be done to ensure that all children have access to the healthcare and nutrition services they need to grow and thrive.

Right to Have a Family Environment, Love, and Trustful People Around

The right to a family environment, love, and trustful relationships is a crucial aspect of a child's development and well-being. It is recognized by the United Nations Convention on the Rights of the Child (CRC) as an essential component of a child's right to life, survival, and development.

A child has the right to grow up in a family environment and to be cared for by their parents, or in the absence of their parents, by someone who is responsible for them. This includes the right to maintain personal relationships, direct contact and care with both parents, regardless of parent's marital status,.

In addition, children have the right to live in an environment that is characterized by love, security, stability, and respect. They should be protected from all forms of violence, abuse, exploitation, and neglect and should have access to education and opportunities for recreation and leisure. Children should be surrounded by people they can trust, who listen to them and respect their opinions, and who provide them with emotional support and guidance.

Governments have a responsibility to promote and protect this right by creating supportive family and community environments and by providing services and support for families in need. They should also work to prevent violence, abuse, and exploitation and to ensure that children have access to appropriate care and support in the event that they cannot live with their families.

In India, the right to a family environment, love, and trustful relationships is recognized by the Constitution and several laws and policies. The Indian government, through the Integrated Child Development Services (ICDS) program, provides health and nutrition services to children and their families, and the Sarva Shiksha Abhiyan aims to provide universal access to education.

However, despite these efforts, many children in India still face challenges to their right to a family environment, love, and trustful relationships. Child labor, child abuse, and trafficking are still widespread in the country, and many children grow up in poverty, with limited access to healthcare and education.

India has a large public health system, with over 1 million health facilities and a network of health workers. The government also provides free or subsidized medication for several diseases, including tuberculosis, malaria, and HIV/AIDS.

Despite this, access to quality medical care remains limited for many people in India, particularly in rural areas.

Civil society organizations and non-governmental organizations are also working to promote and protect this right in India. They work to raise awareness about child rights, provide services and support for families in need, and advocate for better policies and practices to protect children.

According to the Ministry of Women and Child Development in India, as of 2021, around 20 million children in the country are living without parental care. Many of these children are living in institutions, with limited access to their families, and without the love, stability, and trustful relationships that are crucial to their development.

Additionally, child abuse and exploitation are major problems in India, with a significant proportion of children being subjected to physical, sexual, and emotional abuse. The National Crime Records Bureau reported that in 2019, there were over 44,000 cases of child abuse reported in the country.

Poverty is also a major barrier to children's right to a family environment, love, and trustful relationships in India. According to the World Bank, approximately 21% of the country's population lives below the poverty line, and many children growing up in poverty are at risk of malnutrition, poor health, and limited access to education and other essential services.

In conclusion, while the right of children to a family environment, love, and trustful relationships is recognized in India, much more needs to be done to ensure that all children in the country have access to these essential components of their well-being and development. Many children in India are still denied this right due to poverty, lack of access to education and healthcare, and other factors.

Right to Have Parental Care and Fair Treatment of Parents

The right to have parental care and fair treatment of parents is recognized as a fundamental human right and is protected by international law, including the Convention on the Rights of the Child (CRC). In India, the Constitution of India and the Juvenile Justice (Care and Protection of Children) Act, 2015 also provide for the protection of this right.

Parental care refers to the physical, emotional, and psychological support provided by parents to their children. It is a fundamental aspect of childhood and is essential for children's development, well-being, and overall health.

According to the CRC, children have the right to know and be cared for by their parents, unless it is contrary to their best interests. This means that the state has a duty to ensure that children have access to their parents, except in exceptional circumstances where separation may be necessary for the child's protection.

In India, the Juvenile Justice (Care and Protection of Children) Act, 2015 provides for the protection of children's rights, including the right to parental care and fair treatment of parents. The act also provides for the protection of children from abuse, neglect, and exploitation, and establishes a juvenile justice system to ensure that children in conflict with the law are dealt with in a manner that is appropriate to their age and legal status.

However, despite the provisions in law, the situation for many children and families in India remains challenging, with widespread poverty, limited access to education and health services, and high levels of abuse and exploitation. This can result in children being separated from their parents, either through abandonment or institutionalization, and can also contribute to the exploitation and abuse of children and their families.

Even though the data on parental care is collected by various agencies and non-governmental organizations, however, there is limited data available on the quality and accessibility of parental care for children in India. According to the National Family Health Survey (NFHS) conducted in 2015-16, only 51% of children under 5 years of age in India were exclusively breastfed for the first 6 months of their lives and only 39% of children aged 6-23 months receive an adequate diet. That's why stunting, wasting, and underweight remain major public health concerns for children.

A recent study by Save the Children found that 63% of children in India experience violence at home, including physical, sexual, and emotional abuse. This highlights the importance of ensuring that children are protected from abuse and exploitation in the home, which can have serious impacts on their health and well-being. In conclusion, the right to have parental care and fair treatment from parents is recognized in India and is protected by law. However, much needs to be done to ensure that all children and families have access to the support and services they need to live together in a safe, stable, and nurturing environment.

Right to Education, Play, and Recreation

The right to education, play, and recreation is recognized as a fundamental human right for children and is protected by international law, including the Convention on the Rights of the Child (CRC). The right to education is particularly important, as it provides children with the skills, knowledge, and values they need to develop to their full potential and to participate fully in society. According to the CRC, every child has the right to a primary education that is free and compulsory and to secondary education that is available and accessible to all.

According to the latest available data from the Ministry of Education, the literacy rate in India has increased from 74.04% in the 2011 census to 77.7% in the 2021 census. The government has implemented several policies and programs to promote and protect children's right to education. The Right to Education (RTE) Act,

enacted in 2009, makes education a fundamental right for all children between the ages of 6 and 14 and mandates that all children in this age group have access to free and compulsory education. The act also requires that all schools in India maintain certain minimum standards and provide for the appointment of trained teachers and the creation of teacher training programs.

In addition to the RTE Act, the government of India has implemented several programs and initiatives to promote access to education for children, including the Sarva Shiksha Abhiyan (SSA), which aims to provide universal access to education for children in India, and motivating parents to send their ward to school. These scheme also provides for the free stationery, uniform and food. The Mid-Day Meal Scheme also has been implemented, which provides free meals to schoolchildren to increase their enrolment, focus, attention and finally the attendance in school. The government has also taken steps to address the needs of children with disabilities, including through the implementation of the Inclusive Education for the Disabled at the Elementary Level (IEDL) program, which aims to provide children with disabilities with equal access to quality education.

According to the Annual Status of Education Report (ASER), released by the non-profit organization Pratham, there has been an improvement in enrollment in primary schools in India over the past decade, with 96% of children of school-going age enrolled in primary schools in 2018. However, the same report sadly found that 26.1% of children in Std. 5 were unable to read Std. 2 level text, and 47.8% were unable to do basic arithmetic.

Our children in India do not have adequate opportunities for play and recreation. This can be due to a range of factors, including poverty, limited access to safe and accessible play spaces, and cultural attitudes that prioritize work and academic achievement over play and recreation. The right to play is necessary for children because it is an essential part of their overall development and well-being. Play provides children with opportunities to develop their physical, social, emotional, and cognitive skills and to learn how to interact with others in a safe and supportive environment.

Play is also important for children's mental and emotional health, as it allows them to express their feelings, relieve stress, and develop resilience.

Through play, children can learn about themselves, their world, and their place in it and develop a sense of autonomy and independence. In addition, play and recreation provide children with a break from structured activities, such as school and household chores, and allow them to have fun, be creative, and develop their imagination. Play and recreation also promote physical activity, which is important for children's physical health and fitness.

By ensuring that children have access to safe and accessible play spaces and opportunities for play and recreation, we can help them reach their full potential and thrive. The government of India has taken steps to promote education, play, and recreation for children, including through the creation of public parks and play spaces, and the development of programs that encourage children to participate in physical and recreational activities. However, despite this progress, many children in India still do not have access to quality education, and disparities persist, particularly for girls, and recreational facilities children from economically disadvantaged backgrounds, and children with disabilities.

Right to Be Protected Against Sexual Abuse and Exploitation

Everyone has the right to be protected against sexual abuse and exploitation. This right is especially critical for children, who are among the most vulnerable in our society. Children, in particular, deserve robust safeguards to shield them from any form of sexual abuse or exploitation. This includes the right to be free from sexual abuse, sexual exploitation, and any other forms of sexual violence. This right is recognized and protected by international human rights laws, including the Convention on the Rights of the Child, and is considered a fundamental aspect of children's safety and well-being. Children have the right to be protected from all forms of sexual exploitation and abuse, including child sexual abuse, child pornography, and child trafficking for sexual purposes.

It is the responsibility of states, as well as families and communities, to take measures to prevent and respond to cases of child sexual abuse and exploitation and to ensure that those who perpetrate such crimes are held accountable under the law.

According to available data, child sexual abuse and exploitation is a widespread problem, affecting millions of children worldwide. The exact number of cases is difficult to determine due to under-reporting, but estimates suggest that one in 4 girls and one in 6 boys experience sexual abuse before the age of 18. Child sexual abuse and exploitation can have severe and long-lasting effects on a child's physical, mental, and emotional well-being, including increased risk of depression, anxiety, substance abuse, and post-traumatic stress disorder.

In India, child sexual abuse and exploitation is a serious issue affecting a large number of children. According to data from the National Crime

Records Bureau (NCRB), there has been a steady increase in reported cases of child sexual abuse in India in recent years, with more than 38,000 cases reported in 2020. However, it is widely believed that the actual number of cases is much higher, as many children do not report abuse due to shame, fear, or lack of trust & confidence in their parents.

Child sexual exploitation, including child trafficking for sexual purposes, is also a major problem in India. In 2020, the NCRB reported more than 2,000 cases of trafficking of minors for the purpose of sexual exploitation. The internet and online technologies have made it easier for perpetrators to exploit children, with children from vulnerable communities and backgrounds, such as those living in poverty or in conflict zones, being particularly at risk.

In India, the government has implemented various laws and policies aimed at protecting children from sexual abuse and exploitation, including the Protection of Children from Sexual Offenses (POCSO) Act, 2012, which criminalizes child sexual abuse and provides for the protection of child victims and witnesses. However, implementation of these laws and policies is inconsistent, and there is a need for greater awareness and education on child sexual abuse and exploitation, as well as stronger support systems for survivors.

It is important to note that child sexual abuse and exploitation are preventable and that steps can be taken to protect children from harm. Preventing child exploitation requires a multi-faceted approach that involves multiple stakeholders, including governments, civil society organizations, families, and communities. Some steps that can be taken to prevent child exploitation include:

1. Education and Awareness: Educating children, parents, teachers, and community members about the risks and signs of exploitation, as well as teaching children about their rights and how to protect themselves, is crucial in preventing exploitation. Online platforms and social media

can serve as effective mediums for disseminating the right information to the appropriate age groups.

2. Strong Laws and Policies: Implementing and enforcing strong laws and policies that criminalize child exploitation, protect child victims and witnesses, and hold perpetrators accountable is critical in preventing exploitation.

3. Improved Reporting and Response Mechanisms: Improving reporting mechanisms for child exploitation and ensuring that there are adequate resources and support systems in place for survivors of exploitation is important in preventing and responding to exploitation.

4. Addressing Vulnerability Factors: Addressing the underlying vulnerability factors that make children more susceptible to exploitation, such as poverty, lack of education, and exposure to conflict and violence, can help reduce the risk of exploitation.

5. Enhancing Collaboration: Enhancing collaboration and partnerships among governments, civil society organizations, law enforcement agencies, and other stakeholders is important in preventing and responding to exploitation.

It is important to note that preventing child exploitation requires sustained effort and commitment from all stakeholders and that it is a continuous process that requires ongoing monitoring and evaluation.

Right Against Any Commercial/ Economic Exploitation

Children have the right to be protected against any form of commercial or economic exploitation. This includes the right to be free from exploitation in work, such as child labor, forced labor, or hazardous work, as well as the right to be protected from other forms of economic exploitation, such as trafficking, debt bondage, and slavery. This right is recognized and protected by international human rights laws, including the Convention on the Rights of the Child and the International Labor Organization's (ILO) Convention.

Commercial and economic exploitation of children is a serious problem in many countries and can have severe consequences for children's physical, mental, and emotional well-being, as well as their future prospects. It is the responsibility of states to take measures to prevent and respond to

cases of child exploitation and to ensure that those who perpetrate such crimes are held accountable under the law. This includes implementing laws and policies that criminalize child exploitation, providing support and rehabilitation for survivors, and addressing the underlying socio-economic factors that make children vulnerable to exploitation.

There are a few steps that can be taken to protect children from economic exploitation:

1. Strengthen Laws and Regulations: Governments should enforce laws that prohibit the exploitation of children and hold those who engage in such practices accountable.

2. Raise Awareness: Educating the public and raising awareness about the issue of child exploitation is crucial. This includes educating parents, children, employers, and community leaders about the dangers and harmful effects of child exploitation.

3. Implement Monitoring Systems: Governments and civil society organizations should work together to establish monitoring systems to detect and report cases of child exploitation. This can include regular inspections of worksites, hotlines for reporting cases of exploitation, and community-based monitoring systems.

4. Provide Support for Victims: It is important to provide support for children who have been exploited, including access to healthcare, counseling, and legal services. Rehabilitation programs and support for their families can also help children reintegrate into their communities and rebuild their lives.

5. Private Sector Participation: The private sector has a critical role to play in preventing child exploitation. Companies should ensure that their suppliers and business partners are not using child labor, and they should adopt policies and practices to protect children in their supply chains.

6. International Cooperation: Ending child exploitation requires international cooperation and collaboration. Governments, civil society organizations, and the international community should work together to address this issue and support efforts to protect children from exploitation.

In India, child rights against commercial and economic exploitation are protected by various laws and policies, including the Constitution of

India and the Child Labor (Prohibition and Regulation) Act, 1986. The Constitution of India prohibits all forms of forced labor and prohibits the employment of children below the age of 14 in certain hazardous occupations and processes. The Child Labor (Prohibition and Regulation) Act regulates the employment of children in certain occupations and sets age limits for children working in certain sectors.

Article 24 of our Constitution says that "No child below the age of 14 years shall be employed to work in any factory or mine or engaged in any other hazardous employment." The fundamental right against exploitation guaranteed to all citizens prohibits child labor in mines, factories, and hazardous conditions.

Despite these laws and policies, child labor and other forms of commercial and economic exploitation of children remain a serious problem in India, with an estimated 10.1 million children engaged in child labor according to the most recent National Child Labor Project survey. Children from disadvantaged communities and backgrounds, including those living in poverty, are particularly at risk of exploitation.

One of the landmark court cases in India on child labor is **M.C. Mehta v. State of Tamil Nadu & Ors. (1996),** where supreme court ruled on government accountability, education of children, prohibition of child labour and their rehabilitation.

The Indian government has taken steps to prevent child exploitation, including launching the National Child Labor Project, implementing the National Child Labor Policy, and launching the National Plan of Action for Children. However, the enforcement of these laws and policies remains a challenge, and there is a need for greater awareness, education, and resources to prevent and respond to the commercial and economic exploitation of children in India.

Right for Preferable Administration and Implementation of Child Rights

The right to redress and protection of children's rights is an important aspect of ensuring that children's rights are respected and upheld. In many countries, there are specialized institutions, such as children's welfare commissions, that have been established to protect and promote the rights of children.

The primary role of children's welfare commissions is to monitor and report on the implementation of children's rights. Children's welfare commissions also work to raise awareness about the rights of children and advocate for their protection along with providing support to children who have been subjected to abuse, neglect, or exploitation. They also have the authority to investigate cases of child abuse and exploitation, and to recommend appropriate action to be taken.

In India, the administration of children's rights is the responsibility of several government agencies, including the Ministry of Women and Child Development, the National Commission for Protection of Child Rights (NCPCR), and state-level departments and commissions for women and child development. Let's elaborate on these institutions:

1. The Ministry of Women and Child Development: The Ministry of Women and Child Development is responsible for the formulation and implementation of policies and programs that aim to protect and promote the rights of children. This includes initiatives related to education, health care, and social protection for children.

2. National Commission for Protection of Child Rights (NCPCR): The NCPCR is an independent statutory body that was established to monitor the implementation of laws and policies related to the protection of children's rights. The NCPCR has the authority to investigate complaints of child abuse and exploitation and to recommend appropriate action to be taken.

3. State-level Departments and Commissions for Women and Child Development: In each state of India, there is a department or commission for women and child development that is responsible for implementing policies and programs related to the rights of children. These agencies work in partnership with the Ministry of Women and Child Development and the NCPCR to ensure the protection and promotion of children's rights.

In addition to government agencies, civil society organizations and non-governmental organizations (NGOs) play an important role in promoting and protecting the rights of children in India. These organizations work on a range of issues, including education, health, and protection from abuse and exploitation, and they provide support and services to children and families in need.

Overall, the administration of children's rights in India is a multi-faceted effort that involves the participation of government agencies, civil society organizations, and communities. While there are still challenges to be addressed, India has made significant progress in protecting and promoting the rights of children, and this effort should be continued and strengthened.

It is important to ensure that children's rights are not just written in the legislations and government schemes but are also implemented in practice. To this end, several steps can be taken to promote the preferential administration and implementation of children's rights:

1. Establishing Effective Institutions: Governments should establish institutions, such as child protection agencies, that are dedicated to protecting and promoting the rights of children. These institutions should have the resources and authority to carry out their mandates effectively.

2. Allocating Sufficient Resources: Governments should allocate sufficient resources to institutions and programs that protect and promote children's rights. This includes funding for education, health care, and social services, as well as resources for the administration of justice and the protection of children's rights.

3. Engaging Children and Their Families: Children and their families should be engaged in the administration and implementation of their rights. This includes involving them in decision-making processes, consulting them on policies and programs that affect their lives, and ensuring that they have access to information and services.

Governments, civil society organizations, and the private sector should work together to promote the rights of children. This includes partnering with communities, schools, and healthcare providers to create supportive environments for children. The Governments and civil society organizations should provide training and education to professionals, such as teachers, healthcare workers, and law enforcement officers, to help them understand and respect the rights of children.

Above all a regular monitoring and reporting on the implementation of children's rights is crucial. This includes collecting and analyzing data, conducting assessments, and reporting on progress and challenges. Those who violate children's rights should be held accountable, which includes swiftly investigating and prosecuting the individuals, who engage in violence, exploitation, and other forms of child abuse, through fast track process.

By taking these steps, we can promote the preferential administration and implementation of children's rights and ensure that these rights are respected in practice.

Some Common Offenses Wherein One or Other Fundamental Right of Children is Violated

2.9.1. Child Cruelty

Child cruelty refers to acts of violence, abuse, or neglect inflicted on children. Child cruelty can take many forms, including physical, sexual, emotional, and psychological abuse, as well as neglect, which is the failure to provide for a child's basic needs. Child cruelty is a serious issue that has far-reaching and long-lasting effects on children. Children who are subjected to cruelty are more likely to experience physical injuries, mental health problems, and behavioral problems, and they may struggle to form healthy relationships as adults.

In many countries, child cruelty is illegal, and those who are found guilty of such offenses may face criminal charges and penalties. However, despite the existence of laws to protect children, child cruelty remains a widespread problem, and many cases go unreported or uninvestigated.

Cruelty to a child has been defined under The Children Act, 1960, to mean an act by a person having charge or control over a child who either assaults, abandons, exposes, or willfully neglects the child, or causes or procures him to be assaulted, abandoned, exposed, or neglected in a manner likely to cause such a child unnecessary mental and physical suffering.

This is an offense punishable with 6 months' imprisonment, a fine, or both. A manager of a home for children giving such maltreatment to a child would be liable for harsher punishment of rigorous imprisonment up to 5 years and a fine up to 5 lakh rupees.

Where a child becomes incapacitated or develops a mental illness due to such cruelty, the punishment would extend to rigorous imprisonment up to 10 years and a penalty of 5 lakh rupees. These offenses are also mentioned under section 23 of the Juvenile Justice Act, which is likely to be applied most often to personnel in childcare institutions regulated by the JJ Act.

Cruelty to a child can include anything from beating them or creating mental pressure by threatening physical harm. Section 130 of BNS 2023 talks about the assault (erstwhile section 351 of IPC 1860) and which has applicability in this case.

If you suspect that a child is being subjected to cruelty or abuse, it's important to take action, which can be as follows:

1. Report the Situation to the Authorities: The first step in helping a child who is being subjected to cruelty or abuse is to report the situation to the appropriate authorities, such as the police or child protective services.

2. Provide Support to the Child: If you are able to, you can provide emotional support to the child by listening to them and offering them a safe space to talk.

3. Gather Information: If you are able to do so safely, gather as much information as you can about the situation, including the name and address of the child, the names of any individuals involved, and any other relevant details.

Also, remember that it's never too late to make a report if you suspect that a child is being subjected to cruelty or abuse. By speaking up and taking action, you can help protect a child and get them the support they need. If you have reported the situation to the authorities, follow up with them to ensure that appropriate action is being taken.

In Indian society, people have little awareness of child cruelty. Even yelling at a child or scaring them through visual/verbal signs or gestures can amount to cruelty. Apart from parents, educational institutions and teachers also often believe that physical punishment for mistakes is the only solution to keep a child disciplined. Therefore, cruelty toward children has become an accepted norm in Indian society.

In recent times, however, child cruelty in educational institutions has seen a decline due to strict legislative enactments. But domestic abuse of children often goes unaddressed because children themselves are unaware of their rights. Apart from educational institutions and home, children can be prone to cruelty even from their peers, i.e., other children or another child older in age, in the form of bullying. Bullying means abusing and mistreating someone vulnerable by someone stronger or more powerful.

2.9.2. Domestic Abuse

Domestic abuse can be defined as any type of controlling, bullying, threatening, or violent behavior between people in a relationship to a child. It can seriously harm children and young people, and even witnessing a domestic abuse to some others falls in the category of child abuse. It's important to remember that domestic abuse can happen inside and outside the home, over the phone, on the internet, and on social networking sites. It can happen in any relationship and can continue even after the relationship has ended.

The impact of child abuse on children can be devastating and long-lasting, affecting their physical and mental health, education, and overall well-being. Children who have been subjected to abuse are more likely to experience depression, anxiety, and other mental health problems, and they may struggle to develop healthy relationships as adults.

Domestic abuse can be emotional, physical, sexual, financial, or psychological, such as:

1.   Kicking, hitting, punching, or cutting

2.   Rape (including in a relationship)

3. Controlling someone's finances by withholding money or stopping someone from earning

4. Controlling behavior, which affect a child like telling someone where they can go and what they can wear

5. Not letting someone leave the house

6. Reading emails, text messages, or letters

7. Threatening to kill or harm someone or threatening to harm another family member or pet

It can be difficult to identify if domestic abuse is happening, and those carrying out the abuse can act very differently when other people are around. Meanwhile, children and young people living in such environments may feel scared, confused, and isolated, often keeping the abuse to themselves out of fear or uncertainty. Their silence can stem from not knowing who to trust or how to express what they are experiencing, further complicating efforts to provide them with the support they need. One could observe the following signs that a child has witnessed domestic abuse:

- Aggression or bullying
- Anti-social behavior, like vandalism
- Anxiety, depression, or suicidal thoughts
- Attention seeking
- Bed-wetting, nightmares, or insomnia
- Constant or regular sickness, like colds, headaches, and mouth ulcers
- Drug or alcohol use
- Eating disorders
- Problems in school or trouble learning
- Tantrums
- Withdrawal

Living in a home where domestic abuse happens can have a serious impact on a child or young person's mental and physical well-being, as well as their behavior and this can last into disturbed adulthood. What's important is to make sure the abuse stops and that children have a safe and stable environment to grow up in.

According to various studies and reports, the prevalence of child abuse in India is alarmingly high, and the problem is particularly severe in rural areas and among marginalized communities. The causes of child abuse in India are complex and include a range of factors, such as poverty, lack of education, and social attitudes that condone violence against children. In many cases, children who are abused, come from families with a history of violence, and these guardians may have experienced abuse themselves as children.

To address the issue of child abuse in India, a number of measures have been taken, including the introduction of laws and policies to protect children, the establishment of specialized institutions to address child abuse, and increased awareness-raising and advocacy efforts. However, much more needs to be done to ensure that children are protected from abuse and that perpetrators are held accountable for their actions.

Efforts to prevent child abuse in India should focus on addressing the root causes of abuse, including poverty and lack of education, and on improving the ecosystem of support services to children who have been subjected to abuse. This will require the concerted efforts of government agencies, civil society organizations, and communities to create a safe and supportive environment for children.

2.9.3. Child Begging

Child begging is a form of child exploitation that involves children being used for the purpose of soliciting money or other forms of support from the public. In many cases, children who are made to beg are forced to do so by adults who exploit them for their own financial gain. This can include parents, guardians, or organized criminal gangs.

Child begging is a serious issue that affects the well-being and development of children and has far-reaching consequences for their future. Children who are made to beg are often deprived of education and other basic rights, and they may experience physical and emotional abuse, as well as health problems.

In response to the issue of child begging, many countries have enacted laws to protect children and to penalize those who exploit them. In India, the Juvenile Justice (Care and Protection of Children) Act, 2000, prohibits the employment of children for the purpose of begging and provides for the rehabilitation of children who have been subjected to begging.

The Juvenile Justice (Care and Protection of Children) Act, 2015 (JJ Act) is the primary law for children in the country. As per Section 2 (14) (ii) of the JJ Act, 2015, a child who is found working in contravention of labor laws or is found begging, or living on the street is included as a "child in need of care and protection," among others. As per Section 76 of the JJ Act, whoever employs or uses any child for the purpose of begging or causes any child to beg shall be punishable with imprisonment for a term which may extend to 5 years and shall also be liable to a fine of one lakh rupees. Child begging is very prevalent in many countries and are often an underground or informal activity that is not well-recorded and so, may need a different strategies of trial in court to punish the culprits with lesser direct evidences.

For example, in India, it is estimated that there are over 40,000 children who are forced to beg on the streets, and many more are made to beg in other forms of exploitation, such as forced labor and sexual exploitation. According to the National Crime Records Bureau, the number of cases of child begging reported in India has increased in recent years, with over 1,000 cases reported in 2016. Despite these estimates, the true extent of child begging is likely to be much higher, as many cases go unreported or undetected and there is no single repository to show the actual data. To address this issue, it is important to gather accurate and comprehensive data on child begging, as well as to take effective measures to prevent and respond to child begging, such as by improving access to education and support services for vulnerable children and their families. This may include providing education and training to families and communities, as well as support and resources to children who have been subjected to begging.

Overall, the issue of child begging requires a comprehensive and multi-faceted approach that involves the collective efforts of government agencies, civil society organizations, and communities to protect children from exploitation and to promote their well-being and development.

Seeing a child begging on the street can be a difficult and distressing situation. However, there are a few things you can do to help:

- Don't give money directly to the child: Giving money directly to the child may not necessarily help them in the long run and could even put them at greater risk.

- Consider making a donation to a reputable organization: Consider making a donation to an organization that works to support children in need. This way, you can be sure that your donation will be used to make a positive impact.

- Provide assistance in other ways: If you are able to, you can also offer the child food, water, or a safe place to rest. Providing basic necessities can make a big difference, even if it's just for a short time.

It's important to remember that the root cause of child begging is complex and often involves poverty, lack of education and opportunities, and in some cases, exploitation and trafficking. Addressing these issues requires a comprehensive and coordinated approach. You must do whatever you can do, without waiting for a perfect solution to help.

2.9.4. Injury to an Unborn Child

Injury to an unborn child refers to harm or damage that occurs to a fetus while it is still in the womb. This can be caused by a variety of factors, including medical conditions, environmental factors, or trauma. Examples of factors that can cause injury to an unborn child include:

- **Maternal illness or infection:** Certain medical conditions, such as rubella, cytomegalovirus, or toxoplasmosis, can cause harm to an unborn child.

- **Substance abuse:** Substance abuse, such as alcohol or drug use during pregnancy, can cause injury to an unborn child.

- **Environmental exposure:** Exposure to harmful substances, such as lead, mercury, or radiation, can cause injury to an unborn child.

- **Trauma:** Trauma, such as a car accident or physical assault, can cause injury to an unborn child.

Sections 91 and 92 of Bharatiya Nyaya Sanhita 2023 (Quondom 315 and 316 of IPC 1860) envisage the provisions relating to injury caused to an unborn child. They cover situations where an act is done with the intention of preventing such a child from being born alive or causing the death of a child quickly unborn by an act amounting to culpable homicide.

Section 91 mentions that the "intention to prevent a child from being born alive/to cause it to die after its birth" is an essential fact to be established for the offense committed, except when done in good faith for the purpose of saving the mother's life. An offender under this section shall be liable to imprisonment which may extend to 10 years, a fine, or both.

Injury to an unborn child can be a serious and traumatic event. Depending on the specific circumstances, injury to an unborn child can range from mild to life-threatening and can have long-lasting effects on both the mother and the child.

In some cases, injury to an unborn child may be caused by medical malpractice or neglect, and it may be appropriate to seek legal advice to determine if you have a case for compensation. It is also important to consider the emotional and psychological impact of the injury, both for the mother and the family. Seeking support from friends, family, or a mental health professional can be helpful in dealing with the aftermath of an injury to an unborn child.

If you suspect that an unborn child has been injured, it's important to take the following steps:

1. Seek medical attention immediately: If you think that an unborn child may have been injured, seek medical attention as soon as possible. Your doctor will be able to assess the situation and provide the appropriate care and support.

2. Follow doctor's instructions: The doctor will provide you with information about the best course of action for the unborn child and the mother. Follow your doctor's instructions and attend all recommended appointments.

3. Consider obtaining a second opinion: If you have any concerns about your doctor's recommendations, consider seeking a second opinion from another medical professional.

Be prepared for the possibility of delivery: Depending on the extent of the injury to the unborn child, it may be necessary to deliver the child early. Your doctor will provide more information on what to expect. Taking care of yourself during this difficult time is important. Make sure to eat well, get plenty of rest, and seek support from friends, family, or a mental health professional if needed.

Remember, early detection and prompt medical attention are crucial in these situations. By taking action, you can help ensure the best outcome for both the unborn child and the mother.

2.9.5. Child Bullying and Cyberbullying

A bully intends to cause pain, either through physical harm or hurtful words or behavior, and does so repeatedly. Boys are more likely to experience physical bullying, while girls are more likely to experience psychological bullying.

Bullying is a pattern of behavior rather than an isolated incident. Children who bully usually come from a perceived higher social status or position of power, such as children who are bigger, stronger, or perceived to be popular.

The most vulnerable children face a higher risk of being bullied. These are often children from marginalized communities, poor families, children with disabilities, or migrant and refugee children.

There are 3 distinct features of bullying:

1. Intent: There must be an intent to cause pain or disturbance, whether physical, mental, or behavioral.
2. Repetition: The bullying act is repeated on a day-to-day basis.
3. Power: Some superiority in status, wealth, or physical strength.

Child bullying can take many forms and can happen in a variety of settings, including at school, online, and in the community. Here are some common examples of child bullying:

- **Physical bullying:** This includes hitting, pushing, kicking, or any other physical violence toward a child.
- **Verbal bullying:** This includes name-calling, teasing, threatening, or spreading rumors about a child.

- **Social bullying:** This includes excluding a child from social activities, spreading rumors about them, or embarrassing them in front of others.

- **Cyberbullying:** This includes harassing, threatening, or spreading rumors about a child through technology, such as social media, texting, or online gaming.

- **Racial bullying:** This includes teasing, name-calling, or spreading rumors about a child based on their race or ethnicity.

- **Sexual bullying:** This includes spreading rumors about a child's sexual orientation or making sexual gestures or comments toward them.

- **Material bullying:** This includes stealing or damaging a child's belongings or property.

Cyberbullying is one of the most prevalent forms of bullying, affecting children in various settings, such as school, home, and playgrounds. Cyberbullying is a form of bullying that takes place online or through technology. Children can be vulnerable to cyberbullying, which can have serious and lasting effects on their mental and emotional well-being. If you suspect that a child is being cyberbullied, it's important to take action.

Here are some steps you can take:

1. Encourage the child to talk about their experience and take support: Let the child know that you are there for them and that they can talk to you about what's going on. Listen to what they have to say without judgment and offer them support. Let the child know that they are not alone, and encourage them to seek support from trusted friends, family members, or a mental health professional

2. Save the evidence: Encourage the child to save any messages, emails, or other evidence of cyberbullying. This can be helpful in documenting the situation and taking action.

3. Report the bullying: If the cyberbullying is severe, report it to the appropriate authorities, such as the website or service where the bullying is taking place, the school, or the police.

4. Teach the child about digital safety: Help the child understand how to use technology safely and responsibly, and teach them how to protect their personal information online.

It's important to remember that cyberbullying can have serious and lasting effects on a child's well-being. By taking action, you can help protect the child and prevent the situation from escalating.

2.9.6. Kidnapping & Abduction of Children

Kidnapping in any form curtails the liberty of an individual, thereby impinging on the right to life guaranteed under Article 21 of the Constitution of India.

Kidnapping & abduction can be defined as the taking away or enticing of minor children, i.e., under years of age for males/females respectively, from lawful guardianship without their consent. The objective of the section is to afford protection & security to minor wards from being seduced, harmed, or otherwise exploited by others. Kidnapping is then followed by the intent of such kidnapping, like ransom, prostitution, compelled marriage, slavery, begging, or even exporting out of India. The punishment for kidnapping, abduction, human trafficking, slavery, and forced labor varies and is covered under sections 137 to 146 of the BNS 2023 (formerly 359 to 374 of IPC, 1860).

Kidnapping of children is a serious concern in India, affecting thousands of families each year. According to the National Crime Records Bureau, there were over 40,000 cases of kidnapping and abduction of children reported in India in 2019. In 2023, India reported over 1 lakh cases of kidnapping and abduction, with a significant number of these cases involving children. This represents a significant increase from previous years and highlights the need for continued efforts to prevent and address this crime. Children of all ages can be victims of kidnapping in India, but young children are at a higher risk.

In many cases, the kidnappers are known to the child or their family, which can make it more difficult for law enforcement to locate the missing child. As mentioned above, the motives for the kidnapping of children can vary, but some common reasons include ransom or extortion, forced labor, and marriage or adoption. There are steps that parents and caregivers can take to help protect children from kidnapping in India, including being aware of their surroundings, avoiding isolated areas, and keeping personal information private.

Preventing child abduction in India requires a multi-faceted approach involving multiple stakeholders, including the government, law enforcement agencies, communities, and families. Here are some steps that can help:

1. Strengthening laws and enforcement: India has several laws in place to protect children from abduction, including the Juvenile Justice (Care and Protection of Children) Act, 2015. However, there is a need to strengthen these laws and ensure that they are effectively enforced by law enforcement agencies.

2. Raising awareness: Raising awareness about the issue of child abduction can help prevent it from happening. This can be done through campaigns in schools, communities, and the media to educate people about the dangers of child abduction and how to prevent it.

3. Improving community-police cooperation: Communities and law enforcement agencies need to work together to prevent child abduction. Community members can be encouraged to report any suspicious activity to the police, and law enforcement agencies can work with communities to identify and intervene in situations that may lead to child abduction.

4. Using technology: Technology can be used to prevent child abduction and help recover abducted children. For example, the government can launch a national registry of missing children and make it accessible to law enforcement agencies and the public.

It is important to provide support for children who have been abducted and their families. This can include counseling, legal support, and assistance with the search and recovery process. Families play a critical role in preventing child abduction. Parents and caregivers should be vigilant and aware of the dangers and educate their children about how to stay safe. Families should also be supported to provide a safe and secure environment for their children.

Kidnapping of children is a criminal offense in India, and law enforcement agencies are responsible for investigating and prosecuting these cases. Additionally, there are a number of organizations and initiatives working to prevent and address the kidnapping of children in India, including the Ministry of Women and Child Development and the Child Rights and You (CRY) organization. An offender of kidnapping shall be punished under the BNS with imprisonment of 7 years onwards and a fine.

It will require a sustained and coordinated effort from multiple stakeholders like the government, agencies, police, NGOs, and parents to make a meaningful impact toward preventing child abduction for immoral and illegal purposes.

2.9.7. Child Sexual Abuse

Child abuse refers to any intentional harm or mistreatment to a child under the age of 18, including physical, sexual, emotional abuse, and neglect. Child abuse can have serious and long-lasting effects on a child's physical and mental health, development, and well-being.

Signs of child abuse can include physical injuries, changes in behavior, avoidance of certain people or activities, and difficulty trusting others. If you suspect a child is being abused, it's important to report your concerns to the appropriate authorities, such as the police or child protective services.

Child sexual abuse is a pervasive issue in our society, yet it is not often discussed openly. It is the root cause of several health problems and an array of other consequences. The government has taken initiatives to address the issue by enacting the Protection of Children from Sexual Offenses Act in 2012 (POCSO). However, proper implementation of such laws and policies is needed to curb this social menace. The POCSO Act recognizes that the intent to commit an offense, even when unsuccessful for whatever reason, needs to be penalized as well. The attempt to commit an offense under the Act has been made liable for punishment for up to half the punishment prescribed for the commission of the offense. The Act also provides for punishment for abetment of the offense, which is the same as for the commission of the offense. This includes trafficking of children for sexual purposes.

For the more heinous offenses of Penetrative Sexual Assault, Aggravated Penetrative Sexual Assault, Sexual Assault, and Aggravated Sexual Assault, the burden of proof is shifted to the accused. This provision has been made in view of the greater vulnerability and innocence of children.

According to National Crime Records Bureau (NCRB) 2014 reports, crimes committed against children were observed as 20.1 per one lakh population of children (up to 18 years of age). Crimes against children across India increased by 16.2 per cent between 2020 and 2021, according to the latest NCRB data. A total of 19,000 cases of child rape were reported in the country during 2022, under POCSO Act.

It has been reported that one in 10 children may be sexually abused before their 18th birthday. Even with reducing rates of reported sexual abuse, the public is not fully aware of the impact of the problem. Child sexual abuse is an age-old problem in India, and over the years, cases of heinous acts have been rising, even with a constant fight to eradicate such evil from society.

For the immediate relief and rehabilitation of a child following a complaint, the Special Juvenile Police Unit (SJPU) or local police must promptly take action. As soon as a complaint is lodged, these authorities are required to ensure that the child receives care and protection without delay. This includes arranging for the child to be admitted to a shelter home or the nearest hospital within 24 hours of the report. Furthermore, the SJPU or local police must report the matter to the Child Welfare Committee (CWC) within 24 hours of recording the complaint. The Act places a duty on the Central and State Governments to spread awareness through media, including television, radio, and print media, at regular intervals to make the general public, children, and their parents and guardians aware of the provisions of this Act. The National Commission for the Protection of Child Rights (NCPCR) and State Commissions for the Protection of Child Rights (SCPCRs) have been designated as the authority to monitor the implementation of the Act.

Preventing child sexual abuse requires a collective effort from all members of society. This includes educating people about what constitutes sexual abuse, as well as providing resources and support for families to help prevent abusive situations from occurring in the first place.

It's also important for individuals to recognize the warning signs of sexual abuse and to take action to protect children. If you know or suspect that a child is being abused, it's your responsibility to report it to the authorities so that the child can receive the help and protection they need.

Here are some signs that a child may have experienced sexual abuse:

- **Physical signs:** Bruises or bleeding in the genital area, sexually transmitted infections, difficulty walking or sitting.

- **Behavioral signs:** Regression to earlier developmental stages (such as bed-wetting), acting out sexually, excessive crying, mood swings, and depression.

- **Psychological signs:** Nightmares or night terrors, anxiety, fear of specific people or places, self-harm, or suicide attempts.

- **Changes in behavior:** Withdrawal from friends and family, sudden changes in eating or sleeping patterns, avoidance of previously enjoyed activities.

It's important to note that these symptoms can also be caused by other factors and that not all children who have been sexually abused will display these signs.

However, if you suspect a child has been sexually abused, it is important to report it to the appropriate authorities, such as child protective services or the police. The child may need medical attention and professional counseling to help them heal from the abuse.

Administration and Redressal of Child Rights

As per the NCRB latest report, there has been an increase in cases under the Protection of Children from Sexual Offences (POCSO) Act. There were 47,221 POCSO cases out of 1,28,531 cases of crime against children in 2020 (36.73 per cent). The increase in reported cases could be attributed to several factors, including greater awareness, improved reporting mechanisms, and possibly a rise in the actual incidence of abuse. The COVID-19 pandemic also exacerbated the situation, with reports of child abuse, including sexual abuse, surging during lockdowns when children were confined to homes, often with their abusers. Handling child offenses in India involves a compassionate and comprehensive approach, focusing on protection, rehabilitation, and justice. Though under chapter 2.8, we have gone through the contents of administration of child rights and various preferences which are given in handling of legal process around children right. But Under this section, I intend to spell out various steps (call to action) we all can take as a commoner or parent or neighbours. The government and NGOs run campaigns to educate communities about child rights and how to prevent abuse and exploitation. These campaigns aim to empower communities to protect their children. When a child offense is noted or perceived or reported, one should connect to specialized units like the Special Juvenile Police Units (SJPUs) and Childline (1098) These teams are trained to handle children with care, ensuring they feel safe and supported from the moment they are found.

Irrespective of geography and offence type, we do have following there comprehensive legal protections:

1. Juvenile Justice Board (JJB): the cases related to children rights are handled by a Juvenile Justice Board. This board includes a magistrate and social workers who work together to understand the child's background and circumstances, focusing on rehabilitation rather than punishment. The judicial process for children is designed to be less intimidating. Measures like video testimonies and a supportive environment help children feel more at ease.

2. Child Welfare Committee (CWC): For children who need care and protection, the CWC takes charge. They ensure that these children receive the necessary support, whether it's through temporary shelter, counselling, or finding a safe home.

3. POCSO Act: In cases of sexual offenses against children, the Protection of Children from Sexual Offences (POCSO) Act ensures stringent punishments for offenders and a child-friendly judicial process to minimize trauma for the child.

One can file the complaint of child offence with District Child Protection Unit (DCPU): or connect to State Commission for Protection of Child Rights (SCPCR) or National Commission for Protection of Child Rights (NCPCR)

You can file a complaint with the NCPCR. They address violations of child rights and ensure appropriate action.

- **Website:** www.ncpcr.gov.in
- **Email:** complaints.ncpcr@gov.in
- **Phone:** 1800-121-2830 (Toll-Free Helpline)

Many NGOs work tirelessly to rescue children, provide legal aid, and support rehabilitation efforts. They are crucial in creating a safety net for children in distress. Commoners and Communities are encouraged to be vigilant and proactive in reporting any suspicious activities or cases of child abuse, creating a safer environment for children. If they cannot afford to file complaint directly, they are advised to at least inform to these NGO and monitor their action. Along with these, a continuous training for police, social workers, and judicial officers shall help them stay updated on best practices for handling child offenses with sensitivity and understanding.

Children receive counseling and legal support to help them understand what's happening and to make the process less scary. Once children are ready to reintegrate into society, aftercare programs provide continued support, education, and job opportunities to help them build a positive future. By focusing on these comprehensive measures, we can aim to create a system that not only addresses child offenses effectively but also provides children with the support and opportunities they need to thrive.

SECTION: 3

GENERAL

Introduction – Protection under **Bharatiya Nyaya Sanhita**, 2023 Erstwhile Indian Penal Code, 1860, and many other central & state laws, Information Technology Act, 2000., other special and allied laws. The reference of such Acts shall be mentioned in the specific offense and chapters.

The purpose of this section is to provide information and guidance on the legal system, the practice of law, and its implementation. These are applicable to all, irrespective of age and gender. This content may be used by citizens to stay informed about their rights and obligations. However, the legal field is a dynamic and ever-changing study, and so it's important to refer to the latest laws/judicial precedents and take legal advice from a lawyer, to reach any conclusion.

3.1 Abetment

The simple meaning of abetment is to assist or aid. Abetment, as a legal term, refers to the acts of encouraging, aiding, or assisting another person in committing a crime. It is considered a criminal offense in many jurisdictions and can carry severe penalties, including imprisonment or fines. Abetment can include actions such as providing the tools or resources necessary to commit a crime, encouraging someone to commit a crime, or helping to conceal evidence of a crime. The severity of the penalties for abetment will depend on the specific circumstances of each case and the laws of the jurisdiction in which the crime was committed.

In usual parlance, a person is held to be liable only if he or she has personally committed a crime. However, the concept of abetment says that he who has helped the criminal or provided him with any assistance in any form can also be held to be liable. Abetment is defined and punished under Section 45 to Section 60 of the Bharatiya Nyaya  Sanhita 2023 (quondam Section 107 to Section 120 of IPC 1860). The punishment for abetment depends on the nature of the crime that was abetted and can range from simple imprisonment to life imprisonment.

Here are a few examples of abetment cases and their punishments under the BNS:

1. Abetment of suicide: Section 108 of the BNS 2023 (quondam Section 306 IPC 1860) punishes abetment of suicide with imprisonment for up to 10 years and a fine.

2. Under Section 55 of BNS 2023, Whoever abets the commission of an offense punishable with death or imprisonment for life shall, if that offense is not committed in consequence of the abetment, and no express provision is made under this Sanhita for the punishment of such abetment, be punished with imprisonment of either description for a term which may extend to 7 years, and shall also be liable to a fine; and if any act for which the abettor is liable in consequence of the abetment, and which causes hurt to any person, is done, the abettor shall be liable to imprisonment of either description for a term which may extend to 14 years, and shall also be liable to a fine.

3. Abetment of an offense punishable with imprisonment: Section 56 of the Bharatiya Nyaya Sanhita provides that whoever abets an offense punishable with imprisonment shall, if that offense is not committed in consequence of the abetment, and no express provision is made under this Sanhita for the punishment of such abetment, be punished with imprisonment of any description provided for that offense for a term which may extend to one-fourth of the longest term provided for that offense; or with such fine as is provided for that offense, or with both; and if the abettor or the person abetted is a public servant whose duty it is to prevent the commission of such offense, the abettor shall be punished with imprisonment of any description provided for that offense for a term which may extend to one-half of the longest term provided for that offense, or with such fine as is provided for the offense, or with both.

It's important to note that the punishment for abetment is not limited to the examples given above and can vary depending on the specific circumstances of each case and the laws of each jurisdiction.

According to Section 46 of Bharatiya Nyaya Sanhita 2023 (quondam Section 108 IPC 1860), a person abets an offense who abets either the commission of an offense, or the commission of an act which would be an offense if committed by a person capable under law of committing an offense with the same intention or knowledge as that of the abettor.

- Explanation 1.—The abetment of the illegal omission of an act may amount to an offense although the abettor may not himself be bound to do that act.

- Explanation 2.—To constitute the offense of abetment, it is not necessary that the act abetted should be committed, or that the effect requisite to constitute the offense should be caused.

For example:

(a) A instigates B to murder C. B refuses to do so. A is still guilty of abetting B to commit murder.

(b) A instigates B to murder D. B, in pursuance of the instigation, stabs D. D recovers from the wound. A is guilty of instigating B to commit murder.

It is not necessary that the person abetted should be capable by law of committing an offense, or that he should have the same guilty intention or knowledge as that of the abettor, or any guilty intention or knowledge. It is not necessary for the commission of the offense of abetment by conspiracy that the abettor should concert the offense with the person who commits it. It is sufficient if he engages in the conspiracy in pursuance of which the offense is committed.

The Supreme Court has dealt with several cases involving the issue of abetment. The court has laid down several important principles and guidelines for determining liability for abetment in various circumstances.

A few notable cases involving abetment that have been decided by the Supreme Court of India:

1. State of U.P. v. Babu Ram, (1974) 4 SCC 200: In this case, the Supreme Court held that the offense of abetment requires an intentional act of aiding or assisting in the commission of a crime. The court also stated that it is not necessary for the abettor to be present at the scene of the crime, and that mere presence or knowledge of the crime is not enough to establish liability for abetment.

2. Gian Singh v. State of Punjab, (2012) 10 SCC 303: This case dealt with the issue of abetment in the context of suicide. The court held that there must be a direct and proximate link between the acts of the accused and the commission of the suicide for the accused to be held liable for abetment of suicide.

3. K. Anbazhagan v. State, (2015) 2 SCC 767: In this case, the court held that to establish liability for abetment, there must be a clear and direct act of incitement or assistance in the commission of the crime. Mere knowledge or passive support of the crime is not enough to establish liability for abetment.

These cases demonstrate the complex and nuanced nature of abetment in Indian law, and the importance of carefully considering the specific facts and circumstances of each case in determining liability for abetment. To conclude, the offense of abetment is not only complex but also changes its interpretation depending on the gravity of the offense and the surrounding circumstances. Understanding the intent, actions, and influence exerted by the accused in relation to the principal offense is crucial in establishing legal responsibility under abetment provisions.

Attempt to Commit an Offense

Attempt to commit an offense refers to a situation in which a person tries to commit a crime but fails to complete the crime due to some intervening and obstructing factor or circumstance. In criminal law, an attempt to commit a crime is often considered a separate and distinct offense, even if the underlying crime is not completed. The legislative intent behind criminalizing the attempt of an offense, even though it failed, is to keep society under check and deter people from negative thoughts.

In general, the elements of an attempt to commit an offense are:

1. **Intent:** The person must have the intent to commit the crime.
2. **Preparation:** The person must have taken some overt act or steps toward committing the crime.
3. **Proximity:** The act or steps taken by the person must be close enough to the commission of the crime that it can be concluded that the person was about to commit the crime.

The punishment for an attempt to commit an offense depends on the nature of the underlying crime and the laws of the jurisdiction in which the attempt was made. In some cases, the punishment for an attempt may be less severe than the punishment for the completed crime, while in other cases, the punishment may be the same.

The case of Abhayanand Mishra v. State of Bihar (1961) stands as a landmark judgment in Indian jurisprudence, particularly in clarifying the legal distinction between "preparation" and "attempt" to commit an offence. The Supreme Court of India, through this ruling, provided a significant contribution to the understanding of criminal liability in the context of incomplete offenses. In this particular case the submission of forged documents by the accused, was seen as crossing the threshold of preparation and entering into the realm of attempt. The Court ruled that his actions amounted to an attempt to cheat because they constituted a direct movement towards the commission of the offense. The judgment mentioned the legal principle that the criminal law does not merely punish the completed act of crime but also recognizes and penalizes actions that demonstrate a clear intent and progression towards committing an offense.

In India, attempt to commit an offense is defined and punished under Section 62 of the Bharatiya Nyaya Sanhita 2023 (formerly Sections 511-513 of IPC 1860). It provides for punishment for attempting to commit offenses even if the underlying crime is not completed.

The punishment for attempting to commit an offense depends on the nature of the crime that was attempted and can range from simple imprisonment to life imprisonment. Here are a few examples of attempt to commit offenses and their punishments under the BNS:

1. **Any offence for which the punishment is death sentences**. For example Section 109 of the Bharatiya Nyaya Sanhita 2023 (quondam Section 307 IPC 1860) provides that whoever does any act with the intention of committing an offense punishable with death or life imprisonment, and does any act toward the commission of such an offense, shall be punished with imprisonment for a term that may extend to 10 years, and shall also be liable to a fine. Further section 110 states the punishment for "attempt to culpable homicide not amounting to murder" will be imprisonment up to 3 years, fine or both unless the real hurt is caused during such attempt.

2. **Offenses punishable with imprisonment and which has not been specifically covered under BNS.** So as we noted above, under section 109/110 of BNS, where the attempt to murder and Attempt to culpable homicide has been covered specifically and hence section 62, which is a general provision, shall not apply. If the attempted offense is punishable with imprisonment, the punishment for the attempt to commit the offense shall be imprisonment of any description provided for the offense, for a term that may extend to one-half of the longest term provided for the offense. It's important to note that the punishment for an attempt to commit an offense is not limited to the examples given above, and can vary depending on the specific circumstances of each case and the laws of each jurisdiction.

Let's understand this through the following 2 examples:

1. If X shoots Y with a gun to kill him, and Y dies, then X is liable for murder under Section 101 of Bharatiya Nyaya Sanhita (quondam Section 302 of IPC 1860). But if Y survives with injuries, then X shall be held liable for an attempt of murder.

2. If X makes an attempt to pick the pocket of Y by inserting his hand into Y's pocket, and X fails in the attempt only because Y did not have anything in the pocket, though no real offense was committed, by the workings of Section 62 (quondam Section 511 of IPC 1860), X shall be liable for an attempt to pickpocketing.

In general, a case under Section 62 of Bharatiya Nyaya Sanhita 2023 (formerly Section 511 of IPC 1860) can be taken cognizance of by a magistrate either upon receiving a complaint, a police report, or information received from any person other than a police officer.

With regards to bail, it is possible for a person accused of an offense under Section 62 of Bharatiya Nyaya Sanhita 2023 to apply for bail. The grant of bail in such cases would be subject to the provisions of the Bharatiya

Nagrik Suraksha Sanhita 2023, which provide for the grant of bail in cases where the accused is able to furnish sufficient security and where it appears that the accused is not likely to abscond or commit any offense while on bail.

The specifics of cognizance and bail in each case would depend on the facts and circumstances of the case and the interpretation of the relevant provisions of the Bharatiya Nagrik Suraksha Sanhita 2023 by the courts.

3.3 Criminal Breach of Trust

Criminal breach of trust is a criminal offense in which a person who is entrusted with property or funds, misappropriates or misuses that property or funds for their own benefit or the benefit of someone other than the rightful owner. This is considered a violation of the trust placed in the person by the owner of the property or funds.

Three basic elements of criminal breach of trust are entrustment, misappropriation, and fraudulent intent. In India, criminal breach of trust is defined and punished under Section 316 of the Bharatiya Nyaya Sanhita 2023 (quondam Section 405 of the IPC 1860). The punishment for criminal breach of trust can range from imprisonment to fines, or both, depending on the specific circumstances of each case.

The relevant provision, Section 316 of the Bharatiya Nyaya Sanhita 2023, states:

> "Whoever, being in any manner entrusted with property, or with any dominion over property, dishonestly misappropriates or converts to his own use that property, or dishonestly uses or disposes of that property in violation of any direction of law prescribing the mode in which such trust is to be discharged, or of any legal contract, express or implied, which he has made touching the discharge of such trust, or willfully suffers any other person so to do, commits 'criminal breach of trust.'"

An example of criminal breach of trust would be if a person is entrusted with managing the finances of a non-profit organization, but instead of using the funds for the intended purpose, they use the funds for their own personal expenses. This would be a violation of the trust placed in the person by the non-profit organization and could result in criminal charges for criminal breach of trust.

Another example would be if an employee is entrusted with a company's money for the purpose of paying bills, but instead of paying the bills, the employee uses the money for their own personal expenses. This would be a violation of the trust placed in the employee by the company and could result in criminal charges for criminal breach of trust.

The Supreme Court of India has dealt with several cases involving criminal breach of trust and has established several principles and guidelines for determining liability for criminal breach of trust in different circumstances. Some of the key principles established by the Supreme Court in cases involving criminal breach of trust include:

a.   Dishonesty: The accused must have acted with the intention to defraud or cheat the owner of the property or funds.

b.   Misappropriation: The accused must have misappropriated or converted the property or funds for their own use or for some unauthorized purpose.

c.   Entrustment: The property or funds must have been entrusted to the accused person.

d.   Mode of Discharge: The accused must have acted in violation of any direction of law prescribing the mode in which such trust is to be discharged, or of any legal contract, express or implied, which they have made regarding the discharge of such trust.

The Supreme Court has also held that in cases involving criminal breach of trust, the burden of proof is on the prosecution to establish the elements of the crime beyond a reasonable doubt.

Dishonest misappropriation may not be evident at the first instance or as a matter of proof every time. However, when it is established that the property has been entrusted to a person and that the person had control over the property and provided a false explanation for their failure to account for it, the offense of misappropriation with dishonest intention can be established.

Under Bharatiya Nyaya Sanhita 2023, the offense of criminal breach of trust is a cognizable (cases when police may arrest without a warrant) and bailable offense under Section 316(2) (quondam Section 406 of IPC 1860) but non-bailable under Sections 316(3), 316(4), and 316(5) (formerly Sections 407, 408, and 409 respectively of IPC 1860). The punishment for committing a criminal breach of trust depends upon the type of person who has committed the offense.

1. As per Section 316(2) (quondam Section 406 of IPC 1860): Any person who is guilty of an offense for committing criminal breach of trust shall be liable to imprisonment for a term extendable up to 5 years or a fine, or both.

2. As per Section 316(3) (quondam Section 407 of IPC 1860): When a criminal breach of trust is committed by the carrier, warehouse, wharfinger, etc., the accused shall be punishable with imprisonment for a term extendable up to 7 years or a fine, or both.

3. According to Section 316(4) (quondam Section 408 of IPC 1860): When a criminal breach of trust is committed by a clerk or servant, he/she shall be punished with imprisonment for a term extendable up to 7 years or a fine, or both.

4. According to Section 316(5) (quondam Section 409 of IPC 1860): When a criminal breach of trust is committed by a public servant, banker, merchant, agent, etc., he/she shall be punished with imprisonment for life or imprisonment up to a period of 10 years or a fine, or both.

If you face a criminal breach of trust in India, here are some steps you can take:

- Gather evidence: Collect all the evidence you have to prove that a criminal breach of trust has occurred. This may include receipts, contracts, emails, or any other relevant documents. Keep a record of any communication you have had with the other party.

- Talk to the other party: Try to resolve the issue through discussion with the other party. This may involve addressing your concerns and reaching a mutual agreement.

- Send a legal notice: If you cannot resolve the issue through discussion, you can send a legal notice to the other party. The notice should detail the breach of trust and the damages caused as a result.

- File a complaint with the police: If the other party has committed a criminal offense, such as fraud or theft, you can file a complaint with the police. Provide them with all the evidence you have gathered and the details of the breach of trust.

If you are unsure how to proceed, consider hiring a lawyer specializing in civil cases to guide you through the legal process and filing a civil suit for compensation against the offender.

It is crucial to take immediate action if you face a criminal breach of trust to minimize damages and recover any losses.

Forgery and Cheating

Forgery and cheating often occur together because they both involve dishonesty and deception. For example, a person may commit forgery by creating a fake document, such as a contract, and then use that document to cheat someone out of their property or money. In this scenario, the person would be committing both forgery and cheating.

In general, forgery and cheating are often closely related because they involve similar behaviors, such as deception, fraud, and dishonesty. Both crimes can cause significant harm to the victims and can result in serious legal consequences for the offenders.

Under the Bharatiya Nyaya Sanhita 2023, forgery and cheating are both criminal offenses punishable by law.

Forgery is defined under Section 336 of the Bharatiya Nyaya Sanhita 2023 (quondam Section 463 of IPC 1860) as whoever makes any false document or false electronic record or part of a document or electronic record, with intent to cause damage or injury to the public or any person, to support any claim or title, or to cause any person to part with property, or to enter into any express or implied contract, or with intent to commit fraud or that fraud may be committed, commits forgery. This can include creating a fake document, such as a passport or a will, or altering an existing document, such as changing the terms of a contract or forging a signature. An example of forgery: A picks up a cheque on a banker signed by B, payable to the bearer but without any sum having been inserted in the cheque. A fraudulently fills up the cheque by inserting the sum of 10 thousand rupees. A commits forgery. The offense of forgery is related to documents.

Cheating is defined under Section 318(1) of the Bharatiya Nyaya Sanhita 2023 (quondam Section 415 of IPC 1860) as whoever, by deceiving any person, fraudulently or dishonestly induces the person so deceived to deliver any property to any person, or to consent that any person shall retain any property, or intentionally induces the person so deceived to do or omit to do anything which he would not do or omit if he were not so deceived, and which act or omission causes or is likely to cause damage or harm to that person in body, mind, reputation, or property, is said to cheat. This can include a range of actions, such as making false promises or representations, using fraudulent means to induce someone to act, or intentionally concealing facts. Deceiving means making a person believe what is false to be true or making a person disbelieve what is true to be false by using words or conduct. Cheating can take many forms, but the common thread is that it involves dishonesty and deception for personal gain. For instance, a person may convince someone to invest in a fraudulent scheme by promising high returns on their investment.

Both cheating and forgery are considered crimes against a person's property. They might sound similar to a layman, but they are not the same. Let's see the difference in detail:

- Cheating is mentioned under Sections 318-319 (formerly Sections 415 to 420 of IPC 1860) of the Bharatiya Nyaya Sanhita 2023, whereas forgery is described under Sections 336-344 (formerly Sections 463-477 of IPC 1860) of the Bharatiya Nyaya Sanhita 2023.

- Cheating could also be caused by oral statements or documents and may cause damage or harm to the body, mind, reputation, or property. Forgery is usually caused on a document and may damage the title deed and property only.

- In cheating, the wrong-doer deceives an individual and obtains property or gain, whereas forgery could also be committed by drawing/changing a document.

- Cheating can be committed with or without the awareness of the owner of the property, whereas forgery is committed without the owner being aware.

Overall, cheating is considered a broad offense that incorporates forgery under its ambit, while forgery is often committed for the purpose of cheating. The offense of cheating is cognizable but non-bailable, and the punishment for cheating can range from imprisonment for up to 7 years, depending on the value of the property involved and the severity of the offense. The offense of forgery is non-cognizable and bailable, and the punishment for forgery can range from imprisonment for up to 2 years to life imprisonment, depending on the severity of the offense.

A landmark judgment concerning the offenses of cheating and forgery in Indian law is Sushil Suri v. CBI & Anr. (2011), wherein the managing director of a company, was accused of being involved in a conspiracy to cheat a bank by submitting forged documents to obtain credit facilities. The Court upheld the charges of cheating and forgery, affirming that the accused had conspired to deceive the bank by submitting fraudulent documents, thereby causing financial harm. The case also underscored the serious implications of financial fraud and the role of company directors in such offenses.

If you have been a victim of cheating or forgery, it is important to take prompt action to protect your rights and interests. The following steps are suggested to handle cheating and forgery:

1. Report the matter to the authorities: If you have been cheated or if someone has forged your signature or document, you should report the matter to the relevant authorities. This could be the police, the bank, or other relevant institutions. Provide as much information and evidence as possible to support your case. Taking prompt action can help to protect your rights and interests and may help you to recover your losses.

2. Seek legal assistance: It is important to seek legal advice to understand your rights and the legal options available to you. A lawyer can guide you through the legal process and help you take the necessary steps to protect your interests.

3. Keep records: Keep copies of all relevant documents, such as contracts, invoices, receipts, and correspondence. This will help you provide evidence to support your case if required.

If you have been cheated or someone has forged your signature, do not make any agreements or sign any documents without consulting a lawyer. This could affect your legal rights and make it harder to recover your losses. Handling cases of cheating and forgery can take time. It is important to be patient and work closely with your lawyer to ensure that you are taking the appropriate steps to protect your rights. Both crimes can cause significant harm to the victims and can result in serious legal consequences for the offenders.

Corruption

Etymologically, "corruption" has a Latin origin, and it means to break the trustworthiness and good reputation. It is indeed a menace to society and can be defined as the abuse of power or position for personal gain, often at the expense of others. Corruption can take many forms, such as bribery, embezzlement, nepotism, and fraud, among others.

According to Transparency International's 2021 Corruption Perceptions Index, which ranks countries based on perceived levels of public sector corruption, the average score was 43 out of 100, out of 180 countries. Denmark, New Zealand, and Finland topped the rankings with scores of 88, while Somalia and South Sudan were at the bottom with scores of 12. India's score was 40 out of 100, below the global average, ranking 85th out of 180 countries.

There are several ways in which corruption can harm society.

- Firstly, it can undermine the rule of law and erode public trust in institutions such as the government, judiciary, and law enforcement agencies. When people perceive that those in power are corrupt and can get away with illegal activities, they may become disillusioned with the system and resort to self-help or vigilante justice.

- Secondly, corruption can lead to economic inefficiencies and inequality. When public officials and private individuals engage in corrupt practices, resources that should have gone toward public goods and services, such as healthcare, education, and infrastructure, are often diverted to private interests. This can result in inadequate provision of public services and the widening of the wealth gap between the rich and the poor.

- Thirdly, corruption can have severe consequences for democracy and human rights. When corruption becomes pervasive, it can create a culture of impunity, where individuals in power are not held accountable for their actions. This can lead to a disregard for the rule of law, with a corresponding increase in human rights abuses.

Corruption is a significant problem in many societies, and it can have far-reaching consequences for the well-being of citizens. It is essential to address corruption through effective policies, institutions, and measures that promote transparency, accountability, and ethical conduct among public officials and private individuals alike.

According to the National Crime Records Bureau's (NCRB) data, in 2019, a total of 51,452 cases of corruption were registered in India, and 57,929 people were arrested. These figures represent a decrease from the previous year, when 60,345 corruption cases were registered, and 77,209 people were arrested. According to the Center for Media Studies, a Delhi-based think-tank, corruption cost India about $1.5 billion in 2019. The study also found that about 56% of the households surveyed in India had paid bribes for public services. In a different survey conducted by the Indian chapter of Transparency International, it was found that 51% of the respondents had paid bribes to public officials in the previous 12 months. The most corrupt sectors identified in the survey were the police, land administration, and tax departments.

Despite these challenges, there have been some efforts to address corruption in India. The government has introduced various measures such as the Right to Information Act, the Whistleblower Protection Act, and the Lokpal and Lokayuktas Act to promote transparency, accountability, and anti-corruption practices.

The Prevention of Corruption Act, 1988 (PCA), deals with different forms of corrupt practices. Sections 161 to 165 of the Indian Penal Code 1860 used to deal with corruption, and those sections have been repealed by the introduction of new legislation named the Prevention of Corruption Act 1988. Some of the key provisions that deal with corruption under the PCA are as follows:

- Section 7/7A of the PCA - This section states that any public servant who, by corrupt or illegal means, obtains or accepts any gratification/ undue advantage other than legal remuneration as a motive or reward for doing or forbearing to do any official act or for showing or forbearing to show, in the exercise of his official functions, favor or disfavor to any person shall be punished with imprisonment for a term of not less than 3 years, which may extend to 7 years, and shall also be liable to a fine.

- Section 8 of the PCA - This section states that any person who offers, promises, or gives any gratification to any public servant as an inducement or reward for the public servant to do or forbear from doing any official act shall be punished with imprisonment for a term, which may extend to 7 years, and/or shall also be liable to a fine. Provided that the provisions of this section shall not apply where a person is compelled to give such undue advantage

- Section 9 of the PCA, deals with the offense of giving bribe by a commercial organisation to a public servant. Such commercial organisation shall be punished with appropriate fine and if the director or manger found guilty and in connivance of such undue peddling, he/ she shall be punished with imprisonment from 3 to 7 years and fine.

- Section 11 of the PCA, stipulates that if a public servant accepts, obtains, or even attempts to obtain any undue advantage from any person, without adequate consideration or with no consideration at all, and the individual from whom such an advantage is taken is involved in a proceeding or matter connected with the official duty of the public servant (or any public servant subordinate to them), the public servant shall be liable for imprisonment from a minimum of six months to a maximum of five years.

- Section 12 of the PCA, provides for the offense of abetment of an offense under the PCA. This section states that any person who abets any offense punishable under the PCA shall be punished with imprisonment from 3 to 7 years and fine..

These are some of the key provisions of the PCA that deal with corruption. It is important to note that the PCA is a specific law that deals with corruption-related offenses and provides for stringent punishment for corrupt practices by public officials. Civil society and media have also played an important role in exposing corruption cases in India. Public pressure and activism have led to some significant corruption cases being brought to light and corrupt officials being held accountable.

The incidences of corruption can be reduced by raising awareness, strengthening laws and enforcement, and continuously promoting transparency, technology, ethical behavior, and a culture of intolerance toward corruption.

Overall, corruption remains a significant challenge in India, and more needs to be done to address it. This includes strengthening the legal and institutional frameworks, promoting transparency and accountability, and building public awareness and participation in anti-corruption efforts. Addressing corruption will require a long-term, participative, and sustained effort. Also a positive feedback and reward scheme for whistle-blower and keeping their name secret from public domain, could add to the strength in fighting corruption

Criminal Trespass

Everyone has a right to full enjoyment of their property without any disturbance, and this is the genesis of trespass being an offense. Even though trespass is ordinarily a civil offense for which the defendant can sue for damages, when such trespass occurs with criminal intention, it amounts to criminal trespass. Trespassing simply means an act of entering someone else's property/estate/private space without their permission or authorization. This can include walking or driving onto someone else's land or building, or even remaining on their property after being asked to leave.

Trespassing is generally considered a violation of the property owner's rights and can result in legal consequences such as fines, criminal charges, or civil lawsuits. In some cases, trespassing can also be considered a misdemeanor or felony offense, depending on the circumstances, such as if the person was armed or caused damage to the property.

Under Bhartiya Nyaya Sanhita 2023, criminal trespass is defined as the act of entering into or remaining on someone else's property without their consent, with the intention to commit an offense or to intimidate, insult, or annoy the owner or occupier of the property.

Section 329(1) of the Bhartiya Nyaya Sanhita 2023 states that whoever enters into or upon property in possession of another with intent to commit an offense or to intimidate, insult, or annoy any person in possession of such property, or, having lawfully entered into or upon such property, unlawfully remains there with the intent to intimidate, insult, or annoy any such person, or with the intent to commit an offense, is said to commit criminal trespass and shall be punished with imprisonment of either description for a term which may extend to 3 months, or with a fine which may extend to 5 thousand rupees, or with both.

Entering into the property of another with criminal intent, or entering lawfully but remaining on the property with a criminal intent to harm or cause annoyance, shall both be treated as criminal trespass. Criminal trespass has 4 ingredients:

1. Actual entry: To commit the offense of criminal trespass, there must be an actual entry into the property of another by the accused person. The introduction of any part of the criminal trespasser's body is sufficient to constitute house-trespass.

2. Property: The term "property" under this section includes both movable and immovable property. Wrongful entry into one's car or other movable property would have similar liability as wrongful entry into one's house.

3. The possession of the property should be with the victim and not the trespasser. Ownership of the property is not necessary; mere possession is sufficient to claim criminal trespass against the trespasser.

4. If it is proved that the intention of the accused parties was not to insult, harm, or annoy the owners or possessors of the property, then it would not amount to criminal trespass. Intention is the essence of this offense, and if there is no clear motive to commit the crime, no criminal trespass can be proved.

Here are some examples of criminal trespass under Indian law:

- A person enters someone's property without their consent and steals their belongings. This is an example of criminal trespass with the intention to commit an offense.

- A person enters someone else's land with the intention to cut down trees or start a construction project without the owner's consent. This is an example of criminal trespass with the intention to intimidate, insult, or annoy the owner.

- A person enters a temple or mosque without the consent of the authorities and causes damage to the property or engages in vandalism. This is an example of criminal trespass with the intention to insult or annoy the religious community.

Section 329(2) in The Bharatiya Nyaya Sanhita (quondam Section 442 of IPC 1860) defines house-trespass as: "Whoever commits criminal trespass by entering into or remaining in any building, tent, or vessel used as a human dwelling or any building used as a place for worship, or as a place for the custody of property, is said to commit 'house-trespass.'"

Section 330(1) (quondam Section 443 of IPC 1860) defines lurking house-trespass as: "Whoever commits house-trespass having taken precautions to conceal such house-trespass from some person who has a right to exclude or eject the trespasser from the building, tent, or vessel which is the subject of the trespass, is said to commit 'lurking house-trespass.'"

Section 330(2) (quondam Section 445 of IPC 1860) defines 6 different ways under which house-trespass shall be considered as house breaking:

- If one enters or quits through a passage by himself, or by any abettor of the house-trespass, in order to commit the house-trespass.

- If he enters or quits through any passage not intended by any person, other than himself or an abettor of the offense, for human entrance;

or through any passage to which he has obtained access by scaling or climbing over any wall or building.

- If he enters or quits through any passage which he or any abettor of the house-trespass has opened in order to commit the house-trespass by any means by which that passage was not intended by the occupier of the house to be opened.

- If he enters or quits by opening any lock in order to commit the house-trespass, or in order to quit the house after a house-trespass.

- If he effects his entrance or departure by using criminal force or committing an assault or by threatening any person with assault.

- If he enters or quits by any passage which he knows to have been fastened against such entrance or departure and to have been unfastened by himself or by an abettor of the house-trespass.

If you face criminal trespass on your property in India, here are some immediate steps you may prefer to take:

- Firstly, inform the trespasser that they are on your property without your consent and ask them to leave immediately.

- If the trespasser refuses to leave or becomes aggressive, call the police immediately and report the incident. Provide the police with a detailed description of the trespasser and inform them about the situation.

- Consider taking legal action against the trespasser to recover any damages or losses incurred.

If the trespasser causes any damage to your property, take photographs of the damage as evidence.

If you have any CCTV cameras installed on your property, provide the footage to the police as evidence. If the trespasser is caught and charged under section 329 of the BNS 2023 (quondam Section 441 IPC 1860), attend the court hearings and provide evidence to support your case.

It is important to highlight the provision of Section 41 of the BNS 2023, wherein the right of private defense of property extends to harming the wrongdoer, even to the extent of causing death. Such specific situations are of a serious nature, including robbery, house-breaking after sunset and before sunrise, mischief involving fire or explosives, and theft, mischief, or house-trespass that threatens grievous harm. This section permits the use of necessary force, up to and including lethal force, to defend against these grave threats to property. The provision underscores the balance between protecting property and ensuring that the use of force is justified only in serious and potentially life-threatening situations.

It's important to remember that in situations involving criminal trespass, it's always best to prioritize your safety and call the police immediately for assistance, rather than handling thing on your own.

Hurt, Grievous Hurt, and Battery

The offense of hurt under the Bhartiya Nyaya Sanhita 2023 is defined as causing bodily pain, disease, or infirmity to another person. The offense of hurt is punishable under Section 114 (quondam Section 319 of IPC 1860) of the Bhartiya Nyaya Sanhita 2023 and is classified as a relatively minor offense.

On the other hand, the offense of grievous hurt under the Bhartiya Nyaya Sanhita 2023 is defined as causing such bodily injury that endangers life or causes severe damage to any organ or body part of the victim. In the erstwhile Indian Penal Code 1860, sections 320, 325, 326, 329, 331, 333, 335 and 338, dealt with the punishment for offenses of grievous hurt.

The offense of grievous hurt under the present Sanhita (BNS 2023) is punishable under Sections 117, 118, 119, 120, 121, 122, and 124 of the Bhartiya Nyaya Sanhita 2023, depending on the degree of injury caused.

In contrast to hurt and grievous hurt, the term "battery" is a common law term that has not been used in the Bhartiya Nyaya Sanhita 2023. It refers to the intentional and unlawful application of force to another person, which may or may not result in physical harm. Battery is a crime under the laws of many countries, including the United States and the United Kingdom.

To constitute hurt (battery under English law) as defined under section 114 of the Bhartiya Nyaya Sanhita 2023, it is necessary to cause:

1. Bodily pain,

2. Disease, or

3. Infirmity to another

According to section 116 of the Bhartiya Nyaya Sanhita 2023 (quondam Section 320 of IPC 1860), 8 kinds of hurt are treated as grievous, and those are as follows:

- Emasculation

- Permanent privation of the sight of either eye

- Permanent privation of the hearing of either ear

- Privation of any member or joint

- Destruction or permanent impairment of the powers of any member or joint

- Permanent disfigurement of the head or face

- Fracture or dislocation of a bone or tooth

- Any hurt which endangers life or which causes the sufferer to be in severe bodily pain or unable to follow his ordinary pursuits for 15 days

The provisions contained in section 116 of the Bhartiya Nyaya Sanhita 2023 are general in nature. One conceptual clause of dangerous hurt is borrowed from the French Penal Code. It refers to 3 classes of injuries not covered under any one of the above clauses of section 116. It labels the following hurts as grievous:

(a) Endangers life or

(b) Causes the sufferer to be in severe bodily pain for 20 days or

(c) Causes the sufferer to be unable to follow his ordinary pursuits for 20 days

It is abundantly clear that grievous hurt is a more serious kind of hurt. It must be a hurt of any of the kinds stated in section 116 of the Bhartiya Nyaya Sanhita 2023 and must be caused voluntarily as defined under Sections 117(1) of the Bhartiya Nyaya Sanhita 2023 (quondam Section 322 of the IPC 1860).

Depending on the degree of injury caused, the offense of grievous hurt may be further classified as:

- Section 117 (2) of BNS 2023 (quondam Section 325 of IPC 1860) Causing grievous hurt voluntarily. The punishment for this offense is imprisonment for up to 7 years and a fine, depending on the nature and severity of the crime. The offense is cognizable and bailable.

- Section 118(2) of BNS 2023 (quondam Section 326 of IPC 1860) Causing grievous hurt voluntarily by using dangerous weapons or means. The punishment for this offense is imprisonment for life, or imprisonment of not less than one year and up to 10 years and a fine. The offense is cognizable and non-bailable.

It's important to note that if the offender causes the victim's death by intentionally causing grievous hurt or with the knowledge that such injury is likely to cause death, the offense would be classified as culpable homicide not amounting to murder under Section 105 of the Bhartiya Nyaya Sanhita 2023, which carries a much more severe punishment.

It is important to note that punishment for hurt and grievous hurt is subject to section 122 of the Bhartiya Nyaya Sanhita 2023, which prescribes a reduced punishment of one month and a fine of 5 thousand rupees for causing simple hurt, and imprisonment of up to 5 years and/or a fine of up to 10 thousand rupees for grievous hurt. This section applies in cases where such hurt or grievous hurt is committed due to grave and sudden provocation.

There could be motives behind causing hurt, which are addressed under other sections:

- Section 119(1) of BNS 2023 (quondam Section 327 of IPC 1860): Whoever voluntarily causes hurt to any person for the purpose of extorting from him or any person interested in the sufferer any property or valuable security, or of constraining him or any person interested in the sufferer to do anything illegal or which may facilitate the commission of an offense, shall be punished with imprisonment of either description for a term which may extend to 10 years and shall also be liable to a fine.

- Section 119(2) of BNS 2023 (quondam Section 329 of IPC 1860): Whoever voluntarily causes grievous hurt to any person for the purpose of extorting from him or any person interested in him any property or valuable security, or of constraining him or any person interested in him to do anything illegal or which may facilitate the commission of an offense, shall be punished with imprisonment for life or up to 10 years and a fine. It is a cognizable and non-bailable offense.

- Section 120(1) of BNS 2023 (quondam Section 330 of IPC 1860): Whoever voluntarily causes hurt for the purpose of extorting from the sufferer or from any person interested in the sufferer, any confession or any information which may lead to the detection of an offense or misconduct, or for the purpose of constraining the sufferer or any person interested in the sufferer to restore or cause the restoration of any property or valuable security, or to satisfy any claim or demand, or to give information which may lead to the restoration of any property or valuable security, shall be punished with imprisonment of either description for a term which may extend to 7 years and shall also be liable to a fine. It is a cognizable and bailable offense.

- Section 120(2) of BNS 2023 (quondam Section 331 of IPC 1860): Whoever voluntarily causes grievous hurt to any person for the purpose of extorting from him or any other person any confession or any property, for any purpose referred to in subsection (1), shall be punished with imprisonment of either description for a term which may extend to 10 years and shall also be liable to a fine. It is a cognizable and non-bailable offense.

- Section 121(2) of BNS 2023 (quondam Section 333 of IPC 1860): Whoever voluntarily causes grievous hurt to any person with the intention of thereby preventing or deterring a public servant in the discharge of his duty as such public servant, or with intent to prevent or deter that person or any other public servant from discharging his duty as such public servant, or in consequence of anything done or attempted to be done by such public servant in the lawful discharge of his duty, shall be punished with imprisonment of either description for a term which shall not be less than one year but may extend to 10 years, and shall also be liable to a fine. It is a cognizable and non-bailable offense.

- Section 123 of BNS 2023 (quondam Section 328 of IPC 1860): Whoever administers to or causes to be taken by any person any poison or any stupefying, intoxicating, or unwholesome drug or other substance with intent to cause hurt to such person, or with intent to commit or to facilitate the commission of an offense, or with knowledge that it is likely that such an offense will be committed, shall be punished with imprisonment for up to 10 years and a fine. It is a cognizable and non-bailable offense.

- Section 125 of BNS 2023 (quondam Section 336 of IPC 1860): Whoever does any act so rashly or negligently as to endanger human life or the personal safety of others, shall be punished with imprisonment of either description for a term which may extend to 3 months or with a fine which may extend to 2 thousand 5 hundred rupees, or with both. It is a cognizable and bailable offense.

Section 125 (a) BNS 2023 (Quondam Section 337 of IPC 1860): (where hurt to any person by doing any act so rashly or negligently as to endanger human life or the personal safety of others is caused, shall be punished with imprisonment of either description for a term which may extend to 6 months, or with a fine which may extend to Rs. 5000 (5 thousand rupees), or with both.); Section 125 (b) BNS 2023 (Quondam Section 338 of IPC 1860): where grievous hurt is caused, shall be punished with imprisonment of either description for a term which may extend to 3 years, or with a fine which may extend to 10 thousand rupees, or with both. It is a cognizable and bailable offense.

Basically, all the provisions here are related to causing bodily harm of a certain degree under certain circumstances, and the punishment varies with the degree and intent behind causing harm. If you ever face such hurt or grievous hurt, you should first seek medical help and then file a police complaint. If you file a police complaint first, you must get your medical examination done and recorded in the police report even before consulting your lawyer. It's beneficial to collect evidence in the form of an eyewitness or photographs of wounds.

In a recent judgment, the Hon. Supreme Court, in the case of Rohit Chaudhary vs. Vipul Ltd. (2024), held the company liable for the actions of its security personnel under vicarious liability. The case involved allegations of physical assault by security personnel of Vipul Ltd. against the plaintiff. The court ordered compensation to the plaintiff for the physical and mental agony suffered.

Theft, Robbery, and Extortion

Theft and robbery are both criminal offenses that involve taking someone else's property without their consent. Theft is the act of taking someone else's property without their consent, with the intention of permanently depriving them of that property. The property can be movable or immovable, and theft can be committed in various ways, such as stealing, embezzlement, or fraud. The offenses of theft, robbery, and extortion come under Chapter XVII of the Bharatiya Nyaya Sanhita 2023 under offenses Against Property.

Under section 303 of the Bharatiya Nyaya Sanhita 2023 (Quondam Section 378 of IPC 1860), theft has been defined to mean an act of intending to take dishonestly any movable property out of the possession of any person without that person's consent; moving that property in order to such taking is said to commit theft.

Taking the property out of the possession of a person, even temporarily, will constitute theft. However, if the property is taken out of possession of the person just for causing some mental anxiety or in a bona fide perception of the property as one's own, it shall not constitute the criminal offense of

theft. Also, Illustration (g) of the Section explains that one cannot steal property that is in nobody's possession. This concept has also been applied to dead bodies, as they don't have any particular possession. Therefore, trespassing a burial place and indignity to buried body will not come under the definition of Section 303. However, its criminalization has been given effect under section 301 (quondam section 297 of IPC) of the Act, which deals with offering indignity to a human corpse.

Anything that is attached to the earth cannot be subject to theft because it is not movable property in the first place. However, anything that is severed from the earth, at that moment itself becomes movable property, and the act of severing it is, in itself, tantamount to theft. For example, a heavy machine attached to the earth in the first place is not subject to theft, but as soon as it is uninstalled and severed from the earth, it becomes movable property. The offense of theft is punishable with imprisonment for up to 3 years, or with a fine, or with both. The punishment can be more severe if the theft involves a high-value property or if the offender is a repeat offender. For instance, if during the commission of theft the offender loads a gun with the intention of shooting should the victim resist, the act transcends a mere theft. Such conduct would be treated under Section 307, involving the attempt to commit murder, which is punishable by rigorous imprisonment of up to 10 years. On the other hand, robbery is a more serious offense than theft. It involves the use of force, violence, or the threat of force or violence to take someone else's property. Robbery is not just about taking the property, but also about causing fear or harm to the victim.

Under the Bharatiya Nyaya Sanhita 2023, robbery has been defined under section 309 (Quondam section 390 of IPC 1860) to mean an offense of theft or an attempt to commit theft, voluntarily causing or attempting to cause any person:

- Death or
- Hurt or
- Wrongful restraint
- Or fear of either of these

Even after a theft incident has been completed, the commission of death, hurt, or wrongful restraint will give rise to robbery. For example, if a person, after removing the property from possession, slaps the appellant or explodes any explosive or puts the person at gunpoint to scare them so they do not alarm the people in the vicinity and follow the offender, it will amount to robbery under the Section. The offense is cognizable, non-bailable, and non-compoundable.

The offense of robbery is punishable with imprisonment for up to 10 years, or with imprisonment for life, and also a fine. If the robbery involves the use of a deadly weapon or causes grievous hurt to the victim, the punishment can be even more severe. If committed on the highway between sunset and sunrise, the imprisonment may go up to 14 years, as stated under section 309 (4) (erstwhile section 392 of IPC 1860). Punishment for attempting to commit robbery is up to 7 years, as laid down in section 309 (5) (erstwhile section 393 of IPC 1860).

In summary, while both theft and robbery involve taking someone else's property without their consent, robbery involves the use of force or violence and is considered a more serious offense under the law.

Extortion is a criminal offense in India that involves the use of threats or violence to obtain money, property, or other valuable assets from another person. It is a serious offense under Indian law and is punishable by imprisonment and fines. In India, extortion and its implications are covered under Section 309 of the Bharatiya Nyaya Sanhita 2023. According to this section, extortion is defined as the act of intentionally putting a person in fear of injury to his or her person, reputation, or property to compel that person to deliver any property or valuable security or to do anything against his or her will.

Under Section 308(2) of the Bharatiya Nyaya Sanhita 2023 (Quondam section 384 of IPC 1860), the punishment for extortion can be imprisonment for a term of up to 7 years, or a fine, or both. If the person committing the offense is a public servant or a member of an organized crime syndicate, the punishment can be more severe.

According to data published in 2019 by the National Crime Records Bureau (NCRB) in India, the reported cases of these crimes against property are as follows:

1. Theft: In 2019, a total of 521,395 cases of theft were reported in India, which is a decrease of 2.3% compared to the previous year. Uttar Pradesh reported the highest number of theft cases (138,476), followed by Maharashtra (64,079) and Madhya Pradesh (54,623).

2. Robbery: In 2019, a total of 41,761 cases of robbery were reported in India, which is a decrease of 4.2% compared to the previous year. Uttar Pradesh reported the highest number of robbery cases (7,032), followed by Bihar (5,393) and Maharashtra (4,542).

3. Extortion: In 2019, a total of 7,726 cases of extortion were reported in India, which is an increase of 1.9% compared to the previous year. Uttar Pradesh reported the highest number of extortion cases (2,557), followed by Maharashtra (1,141) and Bihar (792).

Even the latest data published by NCRB in 2022, indicates more than 5 lakh cases of theft, more than 30,000 cases of robbery and more than 8000 case of extortion. In recent years, there have been several high-profile cases of extortion in India, particularly in the realms of politics and business. The use of technology, such as social media and messaging apps, has also made it easier for criminals to commit extortion, and law enforcement agencies have been working to combat these crimes through increased surveillance and stricter enforcement of the law.

It is important to note that these statistics may not reflect the actual number of theft, robbery, and extortion cases in India, as many cases may go unreported due to various reasons such as fear of reprisals, lack of trust in the justice system, or cultural factors. Also, the data only reflects reported cases and does not include cases that were not reported to the police.

Marriage-Related Offenses

Marriage is a universal social institution established by human society to control and regulate the domestic life of man and woman. Marriage, as per nearly all religions, is the unification of 2 soul mates who are bound by the virtue of their God or by the laws of the land to live together for life, share grief and happiness, and also procreate children. It is in the family that children learn what is expected of them in society, how to behave, and how to carry out their lives on earth. We need to promote and protect marriage to secure a healthier life and future generations. We, Homo sapiens, being social animals, always need a soul mate, and this unification is celebrated at large in society to create an extra force against separation of married couples, whether physically, emotionally, and even morally.

The above expectation of religion and society gives rise to offenses that originate from the disobedience of the above obligation toward each other. Marriages are, of course, defined legally as well, and even though our Constitution does not define the right to marriage as a fundamental right, a necessary extension of Articles 19 and 21 of the Constitution makes the right to marry the partner of choice seem very obvious. The Indian judiciary has, time and again, stated that the right to marry and the right to a partner of one's choice are part of the right to life and personal liberty under Article 21 of the Constitution.

Marriage is a legally and socially sanctioned union between a man and a woman, regulated by laws, rules, customs, beliefs, and attitudes that prescribe the rights and duties of the partners. The right to marriage does find a place in international covenants like the Universal Declaration of Human Rights, the International Covenant on Civil and Political Rights, etc. So when there is a right, it has to be balanced by some obligation, both toward the spouse as well as society at large. The Bharatiya Nyaya Sanhita 2023 provides for various marriage-related offenses from Section 80 to 87 (Erstwhile Indian Penal Code 1860 addresses marriage-related offenses under Chapter XX). Section 80 of the BNS 2023 talks about Dowry Death (Erstwhile 304 B), Section 81 talks about Cohabitation caused by a man deceitfully inducing the belief of lawful marriage (erstwhile Section 493 of IPC 1860), Section 82 talks about marrying again during the lifetime of the husband or wife (erstwhile Section 494 of IPC 1860), Section 83 (Erstwhile Section 496 of IPC 1860) talks about marriage ceremony fraudulently celebrated without lawful marriage. Section 84 (erstwhile Section 498 of IPC 1860) talks about enticing or taking away or detaining with criminal intent a married woman. Section 85 (Erstwhile Section 498 A of IPC 1860) talks about the husband or relative of the husband of a woman subjecting her to cruelty. Section 86 (Erstwhile Section 498 A of IPC 1860) talks about cruelty. Section 87 (erstwhile Section 366 of IPC 1860) addresses kidnapping, abducting, or inducing a woman to compel her marriage, etc.

Provisions of the BNS are as follows:

Section 81 (Quondam Section 493 of IPC 1860) punishes a man who deceives a woman into having sexual intercourse with him under the pretext that she is married to him, with a ten-year jail term and a fine. The offense is non-cognizable and non-bailable.

Mock marriages, inherently (subject to section 83 of BNS) are not punishable by law as long as they do not involve any illegal activities or actions that violate the rights of others. However, it is important to note that any act that involves dishonest intention, deceit or fraud may be punishable under Indian law. Additionally, consider the cultural and social implications of mock marriages celebrations. Some communities may view mock marriages as disrespectful or inappropriate, especially if they are performed in a public or religious setting. Therefore, it is advisable to exercise sensitivity and caution while planning an engagement, live-in or courtship ceremony in India.

This section is intended to protect women from fraudulent and deceitful men who induce them into a sexual relationship by falsely promising marriage. It is also intended to discourage men from engaging in extramarital affairs and other forms of sexual misconduct. It is important to note that consent obtained by fraud or deceit is not valid, and any sexual relationship based on such consent is illegal. Therefore, Section 81 (Quondam Section 493 of IPC 1860) of the BNS plays an important role in safeguarding the rights of women and upholding the principles of justice and equality.

Section 82(1) (Quondam Section 494 of IPC 1860) talks about bigamy, which means an offense of a person (note that it includes the husband as well as the wife) marrying someone else while still being married to another person. The offense is non-cognizable but bailable, and the offender can be imprisoned for a maximum period of 7 years and fined.

It is important to note that the law recognizes only one valid marriage at a time. Therefore, if a person is already married and wants to marry someone else, they must first obtain a divorce or annulment of their previous marriage before entering into a new one. The offense of bigamy is taken very seriously in India and is considered a grave violation of the sanctity of marriage. The law seeks to protect the rights of individuals and prevent them from being deceived or exploited in matters of marriage. It is advisable for individuals to ensure that they are not committing bigamy before entering into any marriage, and to take necessary legal steps to dissolve any previous marriages before marrying again.

Section 82 (2) (Quondam Section 495 of IPC 1860) states that whoever commits the offense defined in section 82 (1) above, having concealed from the person with whom the subsequent marriage is contracted, the fact of the former marriage, shall be punished with imprisonment of either description for a term which may extend to 10 years and shall also be liable to a fine. The offense is non-cognizable and bailable.

Section 83 (Quondam Section 496 of IPC 1860) states that whoever, dishonestly or with fraudulent intention, goes through the ceremony of being married, knowing that he is not thereby lawfully married, shall be punished with imprisonment of either description for a term which may extend to 7 years and shall also be liable to a fine. The offense is non-cognizable and bailable.

Section 84 (Quondam Section 498 of IPC 1860) states that whoever takes or entices away any woman who is, and whom he knows or has reason to believe to be, the wife of any other man, with the intent that she may have illicit intercourse with any person, or conceals or detains with that intent any such woman, shall be punished with imprisonment of either description for a term which may extend to 2 years, or with fine, or with both.

In 2018, the Supreme Court of India struck down Section 497 (adultery) of the IPC as unconstitutional and violative of the fundamental rights of equality and privacy. The Court held that the law treated women as the property of their husbands and violated their dignity and autonomy. Therefore, adultery is no longer a criminal offense in India. However, it is important to note that adultery may still carry some civil and personal consequences, such as divorce, separation, or damage to reputation. It is advisable to exercise discretion and respect the sanctity of marriage and the rights of all individuals involved. While pronouncing the judgment, the Court observed that any provision asserting the husband as the master of the wife and treating women with inequality cannot be considered constitutional. The decision of the Supreme Court was lauded across horizons, with lawyers and activists welcoming the decision to strike down the antiquated law treating women as the properties of their husbands.

Further, the abetment of suicide of a married woman is addressed under Section 86 of BNS 2023, and dowry death (Section 80 of BNS 2023 and Section 86 of BNS 2023) has been covered in detail in section A of this book.

Matrimonial offenses are multi-dimensional in nature and go beyond culture, religion, caste, and economic status. Matrimonial problems in India are complex and multi-faceted, and it is difficult to provide an exact number of cases or statistics. However, there have been some studies and reports that shed light on the prevalence and nature of matrimonial issues in India. For example, according to data from the National Crime Records Bureau (NCRB), the divorce rate in India increased from 1.1 per 1,000 marriages in 2006 to 1.6 per 1,000 marriages in 2016. According to a national survey conducted by the Ministry of Women and Child Development, 31% of ever-married women in India have experienced physical, sexual, or emotional violence by their spouse or partner at some point in their life. While adultery is no longer a criminal offense in India, it is still a significant issue in many marriages. According to a survey conducted by Gleeden (a dating app for married people), more than 50% of married Indians have cheated on their spouse at some point.

Overall, matrimonial problems in India are complex and varied, and they require a nuanced and multi-faceted approach to address. It is important to create a supportive and empowering environment for individuals and couples who are experiencing marital issues and to work toward creating a culture of respect, equality, and mutual understanding in all relationships.

The literal meaning of intimidation is "to intimidate or threaten a person to do or abstain from doing something as per the choice of the person acting to influence the victim." The act of intimidation can be through the usage of words, signals, or other mental tactics or other indirect dissemination of such threatening communication. Threatening can be done either to cause injury to a person, to cause injury to his reputation, to cause injury to his property, or to cause injury to another person or the reputation of anybody in whom the victim is interested. By including the persons who may be of interest to the victim, the coverage of the offense has been widened. In simple terms, it refers to any warning or threat given to the victim's son, daughter, wife, or any other close family member. Moreover, the explanation mentioned in Bharatiya Nyaya Sanhita 2023 asserts that a threat to harm a dead person's reputation is also protected by this section.

The laws related to criminal intimidation, insult, and annoyance are contained in Sections 351 to 355 of Bharatiya Nyaya Sanhita 2023 (erstwhile Sections 503-510 of the Indian Penal Code 1860).

Section 351 (Quondam 503 of IPC 1860) - This section defines the offense of criminal intimidation, which means threatening someone to cause them to do something they are not legally bound to do, or to refrain from doing something they are legally bound to do. The threat must be with the intention of causing alarm to the person to whom the threat

is made. The person making the threat must also have the intention to compel the person to whom the threat is made to do something that he/she is not legally bound to do or to refrain from doing something that he/she is legally bound to do. The punishment for an offense under Section 351 of Bharatiya Nyaya Sanhita 2023 can be imprisonment for a term which may extend to 2 years, or with fine, or both. The offense is non-bailable, which means that the accused cannot be released on bail as a matter of right; bail can only be granted at the discretion of the court. So, the main components of Section 351 are threats and the intent to cause harm. The threat must be communicated to the victim and this can be communicated verbally, in writing, or even through expressions. Besides that, if there isn't any intent to cause harm, the threat is said to be insufficient. This requirement of criminal intimidation might even be met if the threat frightens the complainant as actual physical harm is not necessary. Physical damage alone must be taken into account for this Section, and mental or emotional trauma may be avoided.

Section 351 (3) (Quondam section 506 of IPC 1860): This section deals with the offense of criminal intimidation by threat of injury to a person or property. It covers cases where the threat is to cause death or grievous hurt, or to cause the destruction of any property by fire, or to commit any offense punishable with death or imprisonment for life. If the threat is to cause death or grievous hurt, or to cause the destruction of any property by fire, the punishment can be imprisonment for a term that may extend to 7 years and also include a fine. It is important to note that criminal intimidation is a non-bailable offense, meaning that the accused cannot be released on bail as a matter of right. Bail can only be granted at the discretion of the court.

Section 351 (4) (Quondam section 507 of IPC 1860) mentions a more serious or agitated type of criminal intimidation wherein the identity of the criminal intimidator is anonymous. The main distinguishing feature of this offense is that the accused commits the offense anonymously without revealing their identity. This offense is punishable by imprisonment for a term of up to 2 years, a fine, or both. It should be noted that this imprisonment is in addition to the usual punishment for criminal intimidation, which is provided under Section 351(1) of the Bharatiya Nyaya Sanhita 2023. The nature of the offense under Section 351(4) of the BNS is bailable, non-cognizable, and non-compoundable, triable by a first-class magistrate.

Section 352 (Quondam section 504 of IPC 1860) - This section deals with the offense of intentional insult with the intent to provoke a breach of peace, which means intentionally insulting someone in a way that is likely to cause a breach of peace and the accused are punished with imprisonment up to 2 years. Unlike Section 351, under this section, physical harm and the purpose of causing damage are not essential for the offense. So, when someone intentionally insults and instigates the victim (for example, by using offensive language or abuse for a family member), the offender must be aware that his instigation may induce the victim to disrupt public order or commit an offense punishable under law.

Section 353 (Quondam section 505 of IPC 1860) - This section deals with the offense of making statements that create or promote enmity, hatred, or ill-will between different groups on the basis of religion, race, language, caste, etc. The section has 3 parts:

- Section 353 (a) (Quondam section 505 (1) of IPC 1860) talks about making, publishing, or circulating any statement, false information, rumor, or report, including through electronic means, with intent to cause, or which is likely to cause, any officer, soldier, sailor, or airman in the Army, Navy, or Air Force of India to mutiny or otherwise disregard or fail in his duty as such; or

- Section 353 (b) talks about making, publishing, or circulating any statement, false information, rumor, or report, including through electronic means, with intent to cause, or which is likely to cause, fear or alarm to the public, or to any section of the public, whereby any person may be induced to commit an offense against the State or against the public tranquility; or

- Section 353 (c) talks about making, publishing, or circulating any statement, false information, rumor, or report, including through electronic means, with intent to incite, or which is likely to incite, any class or community of persons to commit any offense against any other class or community.

The punishment for an offense under Section 353 of Bharatiya Nyaya Sanhita can be imprisonment for a term which may extend to 3 years, or with fine, or both. The offense is non-bailable and cognizable, which means that the accused can be arrested without a warrant. The punishment can be more severe(up to five years of imprisonment) if the offense is committed with the intent to incite a riot or cause violence between different groups or is done inside a religious worship place.

Section 354 (Quondam section 508 of IPC 1860) states that whoever voluntarily causes or attempts to cause any person to do anything which that person is not legally bound to do, or to omit to do anything which they are legally entitled to do, by inducing or attempting to induce that person to believe that they or any person in whom they are interested will become or will be rendered by some act of the offender an object of Divine displeasure if they do not do the thing which it is the object of the offender to cause them to do, or if they do the thing which it is the object of the offender to cause them to omit, shall be punished with imprisonment of either description for a term which may extend to one year, or with a fine, or with both.

For example:

(a) A throws some colored rice, some object, or simply sits at Z's door with the intention of causing it to be believed that, by doing so, they render

Z an object of Divine displeasure. A has committed the offense defined in this section.

The offense under this section is non-cognizable, bailable, triable by any magistrate, and compoundable by the person against whom the offense was committed.

It is very important to understand the difference between criminal intimidation and the similarly sounding offense of extortion (section 308). These 2 terms are generally used commonly but are not the same. Extortion has a very distinct feature wherein the demand/delivery of money or any other valuable security is a prime component of the offense, unlike criminal intimidation. Also, in extortion, both constructive as well as actual force should be used, whereas the offense of criminal intimidation only requires constructive force.

So, looking at the above section, should we interpret that if anyone threatens, we can go and file an FIR? The answer is a subtle no. A simple threat and criminal intimidation are both related to causing fear or apprehension in another person, but there is a subtle difference between the 2.

A threat is a statement or action that suggests the possibility of harm or danger to another person or their property. A threat can be made with or without the intention of causing harm, and it may or may not be unlawful. For example, a person may threaten to sue someone in court for not fulfilling a contractual obligation or stopping someone from doing an unlawful act like property trespassing. Such a threat is not necessarily unlawful or criminal in nature.

Criminal intimidation, on the other hand, involves the use of threats or intimidation to compel someone to do something they are not legally bound to do, or to refrain from doing something they are legally entitled to do. In other words, criminal intimidation involves a threat with the intention of causing the victim to act in a certain way or to refrain from acting in a certain way. The threat must be of such a nature that it is likely to cause alarm or fear in the victim.

In summary, while both a threat and criminal intimidation involve the use of statements or actions that cause fear or apprehension in another person, the quantum and use of such fear is important to judge whether it is a simple threat or criminal intimidation.

If someone threatens you or your family member, it is important to analyze the seriousness of such a threat (who made it, any background, and for what reason) and take appropriate steps to ensure your safety. If the threat seems serious and grave, it is pertinent to document it, like keeping phone call records or screenshots, and inform the police to take appropriate safety measures.

Public Nuisance & Misconduct By Intoxicated Persons

Chapter XV of the **Bharatiya Nyaya Sanhita (BNS) 2023**, encompassing Sections 270 to 297, addresses public nuisance and offenses affecting public health, safety, convenience, decency, and morals. A person is considered guilty of public nuisance if they commit an act or engage in an illegal omission that causes common injury, danger, or annoyance to the public or the general populace. The provisions under this chapter include a range of offenses such as spreading infectious diseases, disobeying quarantine regulations, adulterating and selling food or drugs, and engaging in negligent driving, among others. These laws are designed to protect the community by ensuring that actions harmful to public well-being are appropriately penalized. Nuisance could be defined as unlawful interference in the peaceful enjoyment of one's property or any right associated with it. Nuisance could occur either concerning a particular individual's property rights or in the context of the general public's property rights or any other right which gets indirectly affected. For example, playing high-pitched sound in a place where there are other people as well might amount to nuisance, even though no one is targeted.

Section 270 of the Bharatiya Nyaya Sanhita **(Quondam section 268 of IPC 1860)** makes it an offense to commit a public nuisance, which includes any act that causes annoyance or injury to the public or any person in general. This provision can be applied to cases where an Intoxicated person is causing a disturbance in public, such as by shouting, fighting, or otherwise behaving in an unruly manner.

Many of these nuisances also stems out of the fact that the offenders are under intoxication and they may not understand the consequences of their acts.

Talking alone about the Alcohol as intoxicant, according to the World Health Organization's (WHO) Global Status Report on Alcohol and Health 2018, Alcohol consumption was responsible for 3 million deaths worldwide in 2016 (2.6 million in 2019), representing 5.3% of all deaths. There is a causal relationship between the harmful use of alcohol and a range of mental and behavioral disorders, other noncommunicable conditions, and injuries. The per capita alcohol consumption in India was 5.7 liters of pure alcohol per person, which is lower than the global average of 6.4 liters of pure alcohol per person.

Toxic liquor consumption is also very common in India and death is often the result of people consuming illegally brewed or bootlegged alcohol, which can contain high levels of toxic chemicals such as methanol, a type of alcohol that is highly toxic and can cause severe harm or even death when ingested. In 2021, for example, at least 86 people died after consuming illegally brewed alcohol in the state of Uttar Pradesh, and in 2022, 42 people died and 97 were critically hospitalized in Gujarat.

The intoxicants including alcohol are not good for health but the problem arises when such intoxicated people cause nuisance in public and harm people and property around them, as they are not in full control of their physical or mental faculties. Misconduct in public by an intoxicated person can have serious consequences for both the individual and the public around them. It is important to address this behavior as quickly and safely as possible to prevent harm to oneself and others.

Bharatiya Nyaya Sanhita contains several provisions related to misconduct in public by a drunken person. These provisions are aimed at maintaining public order and restraining public nuisance.

Section 355 **(Quondam section 510 of IPC 1860)** of the Bharatiya Nyaya Sanhita 2023 deals directly with the offense of misconduct by a drunken person. The section states that whoever, in a state of intoxication, appears in any public place, or in any place where it is a trespass for them to enter, and there conducts themselves in such a manner as to annoy any person, shall be punished with simple imprisonment for a term which may extend to 24 hours, or with a fine which may extend to one thousand rupees, or with both. This section can also be applied where a drunken person is making lewd or inappropriate comments or gestures toward women in public. The offense is bailable and non-cognizable but non-compoundable.

Section 292 of the Bharatiya Nyaya Sanhita **(Quondam section 290 of IPC 1860)** makes it an offense to commit a public nuisance in a case not otherwise provided for in the Bharatiya Nyaya Sanhita. This provision can be applied to cases where a drunken person is creating a disturbance in public, but the disturbance does not fall under the specific categories of offenses listed in other provisions of the Bharatiya Nyaya Sanhita.

It is important to note that this section applies only to cases where a drunken person is causing annoyance to others in a public place and does not cover other forms of misconduct or criminal offenses that may be committed by a drunken person. Other provisions of the Bharatiya Nyaya Sanhita 2023 may be also applicable in such cases.

There have been several cases in India where drunken persons have caused offenses to others in public places. These cases often involve behavior that is disruptive, aggressive, or offensive, and can lead to criminal charges under the Bharatiya Nyaya Sanhita 2023. One high-profile case involved a Bollywood actor who was arrested in 2012 for drunkenly assaulting a businessman in a Mumbai pub. The actor was charged with assault and criminal intimidation under sections 352 (now 131 of the Bharatiya Nyaya Sanhita) and 506 (now 353 (3) of the Bharatiya Nyaya Sanhita) of the IPC, respectively.

In another case, a man was arrested in 2020 for allegedly making offensive remarks and gestures toward women on a Mumbai local train while under the influence of alcohol. He was charged under section 509 of the IPC for intending to insult the modesty of a woman, and section 294 for making obscene acts or words in public. The man was later released on bail.

There have also been cases where drunken persons have caused offenses to religious or cultural sensibilities. For example, in 2018, a man was arrested in Karnataka for allegedly shouting anti-Hindu slogans while under the influence of alcohol. He was charged under section 295A of the IPC for deliberately insulting religious feelings, and section 153A for promoting enmity between different religious groups.

These cases illustrate the potential consequences of causing offense while under the influence of alcohol. It is important for individuals to behave responsibly and considerately in public and to be aware of the legal implications of their actions.

The exception for offenses committed by an intoxicated person is outlined in Section 23 of the Bharatiya Nyaya Sanhita (BNS) 2023. This section states that an act is not considered an offense if, at the time of its commission, the individual was, due to intoxication, incapable of understanding the nature of the act or recognizing that what they were doing was wrong or illegal. However, this exception applies only if the intoxication was involuntary—that is, if the substance was administered without the person's knowledge or against their will.

If an intoxicated person causes an offense to you, there are several steps you can take to ensure your safety and seek redress for the harm caused. Here are some suggestions:

- Stay Calm: If a drunken person is causing an offense to you, it is important to stay calm and avoid escalating the situation. Try to move away from the person if possible, and avoid engaging in any argument or physical altercation.

- Document the Incident: If possible, document the incident by taking pictures or videos, or writing down any details of the person's behavior that may be relevant. This information can be useful in filing a complaint or seeking legal action against the offender.

- File a Complaint and take legal help: You can file a complaint with the police or other relevant authorities, detailing the incident and providing any evidence you may have.

If any such incident has caused you harm, physical or otherwise, you may consider seeking legal help to pursue compensation or other legal remedies. It is always important to prioritize your safety and well-being in any situation involving an intoxicated person, as the person may not fully understand their actions and may be causing trouble unknowingly. The local administration should also look into increasing police presence in areas with frequent offenses, promoting responsible drinking, and enforcing laws and regulations strictly through high fines, imprisonment, and community awareness programs.

Recovery of Money and Bouncing of Cheque

A cheque is used in India as a bill of exchange issued by an issuer bank that is payable on demand. The person who issues and writes the cheque is called the drawer, and the person who receives the cheque and in whose name the cheque is drawn is called the drawee. Cheques could be either account payee or bearer. For account payee marked cheques, you need to deposit the cheque in your own bank account, and the bank shall clear it through the clearing house.

If you submit the cheque at the bank and receive the correct amount, the cheque is regarded as honored. However, if the bank cannot pay the required amount stated in the cheque to the payee, the cheque is then said to be dishonored or bounced.

There are several reasons why cheques may bounce or be dishonored in India. Here are some of the major reasons:

- Insufficient Funds: One of the most common reasons for cheque bounce is insufficient funds in the account of the cheque issuer. When a cheque is presented for payment, the bank checks if there are enough funds in the account to honor the cheque. If there are insufficient funds, the cheque is dishonored.

- Signature Mismatch: Another common reason for cheque bounce is a signature mismatch. The bank checks the signature on the cheque against the signature of the account holder on record. If there is a discrepancy, the cheque may be dishonored.

- Stale Cheques: A cheque is considered stale if it is presented for payment after 3 months from the date of issue. Banks may refuse to honor stale cheques, leading to cheque bounce.

- Technical Reasons: There are several technical reasons why cheques may be dishonored, such as an incorrect date, alteration or overwriting on the cheque, or non-compliance with other legal requirements.

- Account Closed: If the bank account of the cheque issuer is closed, the cheque will be dishonored.

- Post-dated Cheques: If a cheque is post-dated, i.e., it is issued for a future date, the bank may dishonor it if presented before the date mentioned on the cheque.

Even though a money recovery suit and an FIR for cheating under section 318 of Bharatiya Nyaya Sanhita 2023 **(Quondam section 420 of IPC 1860)** could be pursued in such cases of dishonoring of cheques, Section 138 of the Negotiable Instruments Act, 1881, lays down the practical legal provisions related to cheque bouncing.

To make out a case under section 138 of the NIA, 1881, the following components of offenses should be considered:

a. Presentation of the Cheque: The cheque must have been presented to the bank within the validity period.

b. Dishonor of the Cheque: The cheque should have been dishonored by the bank due to reasons such as insufficient funds, account closure, or mismatched signatures.

c. Legal Notice: The payee (the person to whom the cheque was issued) must have served a legal notice demanding payment within 30 days of the receipt of the dishonored cheque.

d. Non-payment within the Notice Period: The drawer of the cheque (the person who issued the cheque) should have failed to make the payment within 15 days of receiving the legal notice.

According to Section 138 of the Negotiable Instruments Act, 1881, if a cheque is dishonored by the bank for insufficient funds or any other reason, the person who issued the cheque (the drawer) can be held liable for criminal prosecution. The drawer of a dishonored cheque can be punished with imprisonment for a term that may extend up to 2 years, or with a fine that may extend up to twice the amount of the cheque, or with both. In addition, the payee of the cheque can file a civil suit for recovery of the amount due. As a drawer of a cheque, you must take precautions such as checking your bank balance regularly, issuing cheques by planning funds, issuing post-dated cheques if needed, and maintaining a list of such post-dated cheques along with being acquainted with banking procedures and the time lag for clearing cheques. If the cheque issued by you bounces, you should immediately talk to the payee and replace the cheque or settle the amount and take back your bounced cheque along with the bank memo.

Now let's delve into the process to be followed if a cheque gets dishonored and, as a payee, you hear nothing from the payer. If a cheque issued by your client/payer bounces, meaning it is not honored by their bank due to insufficient funds or any other reason, here are some steps you can take:

- **Contact the Client:** Notify your client immediately about the bounced cheque. It is possible that it was an unintentional error or oversight on their part. Communicate politely but firmly, requesting clarification and a resolution.

- **Re-present the Cheque:** In some cases, the bank may allow you to re-present the cheque for payment. Confirm with your bank if this is an option and follow their instructions on the re-presenting process.

However, re-presenting the cheque is only effective if there is a reasonable chance that the client will be able to cover the amount.

- Communicate in Writing: Send a written notice to the client, documenting the bounced cheque incident and requesting payment. This can serve as evidence in case further legal action becomes necessary.

- Explore Alternate Payment Options: Discuss alternative payment methods with your client, such as a wire transfer, electronic funds transfer, or payment through a different cheque. Be open to finding a mutually acceptable solution to ensure that you receive the payment owed.

- Consult with a Lawyer: If the client does not cooperate or fails to provide a satisfactory resolution, consider seeking legal advice from a lawyer who specializes in contract law or debt recovery. They can guide you on the legal options available to recover the amount owed.

- Assess the Risks and Costs: Before pursuing legal action, evaluate the costs, time, and effort involved. Determine if the amount in question justifies pursuing legal remedies, taking into account potential legal fees, court expenses, and the likelihood of successfully recovering the funds.

- Maintain Documentation: Keep records of all communication, including emails, letters, and copies of the bounced cheque. These documents can be valuable evidence if you need to escalate the matter legally.

When it comes to recovering money through the Negotiable Instruments Act, Section 138, there are several precautions you must take. The top 3 steps/things to be kept in mind for successful litigation are as follows:

- Ensure a Valid Cheque: Make sure the cheque in question meets all the requirements of a valid instrument under the Negotiable

Instruments Act. This includes ensuring that the cheque is properly signed, dated, and contains all the necessary details such as the amount in words and figures, payee name, and bank details. You also need to preserve the cheque along with the bank memo, which states the reason for dishonor, as it will serve as crucial evidence in legal proceedings. Preserve it safely and make copies of it for your records.

- Serve a Legal Notice: Within 30 days of receiving information from your bank about the cheque being dishonored, send a legal notice to the issuer of the cheque demanding payment. The notice should clearly state the facts of the case, the amount owed, and provide a reasonable time (usually 15 days) for the issuer to make the payment. Maintaining and preserving the proof of delivery is again very important, so ensure that the legal notice is sent by registered post or through a reliable courier service with a delivery receipt. Keep the postal receipt or courier acknowledgment as proof of delivery.

- File a Complaint: If the issuer fails to make the payment within the specified time mentioned in the legal notice, you can file a complaint under Section 138 of the Negotiable Instruments Act. The complaint should be filed within 30 days from the expiry of the notice period. Collect all relevant evidence to support your case, such as bank statements, copies of the bounced cheque, the original legal notice, and any other correspondence related to the transaction. This evidence will help establish your claim in court. It is advisable to engage an experienced advocate who specializes in cheque bouncing cases to guide you through the legal process. They can help prepare your case, represent you in court, and ensure compliance with legal procedures. Cooperate with your advocate and try to attend all court hearings if possible, and you must attend when it is required as per court or your advocate.

If you are considering filing a civil suit (other than 138 in NI Act) for the recovery of money, it is highly recommended to consult with an experienced attorney who specializes in civil litigation. They can provide legal advice specific to your case, assess the viability of your claim, and guide you through the legal process. Before you spend any money through legal and attorney fees, you must check the applicable laws and find out if there is a limitation period.

If the suit is not beyond the limitation period (for money suits in general, it's 3 years from the date of the cause of action), then you must evaluate the claim amount, the quality of evidence in your favor, and the overall cost of collection. Here, you must count the loss of your own personal time too, because litigation at times becomes very time-consuming and tiring. In certain cases, the parties involved may opt for the compounding of the offense. Compounding refers to the settlement of the dispute by mutual agreement between the parties, subject to the satisfaction of the court. The conditions for compounding may vary depending on the specific circumstances and the discretion of the court.

In my personal opinion, before you start any sort of litigation for money recovery, you must make sure that all chances of reconciliation and mediation have been exhausted. I also suggest that it is practical to go for out-of-court settlement as well to save time, energy, and at any given point in time, you must evaluate your options and do an evaluation of settlement money and the cost of litigation.

Online Fraud and Cyber Crime

Online fraud refers to any fraudulent activity conducted over the internet with the intent to deceive or trick individuals or organizations for financial gain and loss to such add other individuals or organizations. It encompasses a wide range of criminal activities, including identity theft, phishing scams, credit card fraud, fake online auctions, pyramid schemes, and more.

The malicious incidents related to smart devices (not really smartphones in those days) were first reported in the 1970s when early computerized phones were becoming a target for playing around with the codes and hardware in such a way that long-distance calls were possible by escaping the identity of the caller. Tech-savvy people known as "phreakers" found a way to exploit the system by modifying hardware and software to steal long-distance phone time. This made us realize that computer systems were vulnerable to criminal activity, and as the smartness of machines went up, so did the smartness of phreakers, and devices were more susceptible to cybercrime.

According to the annual "Cyber Security Breaches Survey 2021" by the UK Department for Digital, Culture, Media & Sport, the cost of cybercrime for businesses worldwide exceeded $1 trillion in 2020. The costs of cybercrime can vary depending on several factors, including the size and industry of the targeted organization, the sophistication of the attack, and the effectiveness of cybersecurity measures in place. Factors such as data breaches, ransomware attacks, and intellectual property theft contribute to the financial impact of cybercrime. Overall, many incidents of cybercrime and internet fraud go unreported on multiple occasions.

According to another data from Statista, the FBI and IMF, Cybercrime is a real and growing threat, with the global cost of online crimes expected to surge to $23.84 trillion by 2027, up from $8.44 trillion in 2022.

Factors like higher internet penetration, IoT and smart devices, the growing number of startups, and low budgets for cybersecurity for other SMBs, along with policies like BYOD (bring your own device), contribute further to such online and cybercrimes. Cybercrimes in general can be classified into 4 categories:

1. Individual Cyber Crimes: This type targets individuals. It includes phishing, spoofing, spam, cyberstalking, and more.

2. Organization Cyber Crimes: The main target here is organizations. Usually, this type of crime is done by teams of criminals, including malware attacks and denial of service attacks.

3. Property Cybercrimes: This type targets property like credit cards, bank accounts, payment wallets, or even intellectual property rights.

4. Society Cybercrimes: This is the most dangerous form of cybercrime, as it includes cyber terrorism, propaganda against a particular community, nation, or religions, resulting in unrest in society.

Let's understand some common cybercrimes and their nature before we discuss prevention.

- Ransomware: Malicious software that encrypts victims' files and demands a ransom payment in exchange for decryption.

- Data Breaches: Unauthorized access to sensitive information, such as personal data, login credentials, or financial details, often leading to identity theft or fraud.

- Phishing: Fraudsters trick individuals into revealing sensitive information by impersonating legitimate entities via email, text messages, or fake websites.

- Distributed Denial of Service (DDoS) Attacks: Overwhelming a target's network or website with a flood of traffic to disrupt or temporarily disable their online services.

- Malware: Malicious software designed to infiltrate, damage, or gain unauthorized access to computer systems.

- Social Engineering: Manipulating individuals through psychological techniques to deceive them into revealing sensitive information or performing certain actions.

- Identity Theft: Involves stealing personal information, such as Social Security numbers or financial details, to impersonate someone else.

- Phishing: Fraudsters trick victims into revealing sensitive information by pretending to be a trustworthy entity through email, text messages, or fake websites.

- Credit Card Fraud: Unauthorized use of credit or debit card details to make purchases or withdraw funds.

- Auction Fraud: Scammers create fake online auctions, receive payments for products that don't exist, and then disappear.

- Advance Fee Fraud: Victims are asked to pay a fee in advance for a promised benefit, such as a lottery win or a large inheritance, which never materializes.

- Business Email Compromise (BEC): Fraudsters target businesses by impersonating executives or suppliers to deceive employees into transferring funds or sensitive information.

Fighting a crime committed on the internet or through smart devices can be pursued under various provisions of laws, but prevention and security measures for the above crimes should be taken first to restrict the incidence of occurrences. As responsible individuals or businesses, the following precautions can be taken:

- Strong passwords, regular password updates, and two-factor authentication (2FA) help protect against unauthorized access.

- Regular software updates and patches are crucial to addressing vulnerabilities in operating systems and applications.

- Firewalls, antivirus software, and intrusion detection systems are essential for detecting and preventing malware attacks.

- Employee cybersecurity training, awareness programs, and best practices help mitigate social engineering and phishing threats.

- Secure browsing habits, such as verifying website authenticity and not clicking on suspicious links or attachments, can mitigate phishing attempts.

- Educating individuals and organizations about online fraud risks and providing cybersecurity awareness training is crucial.

Although these crimes are more commonly linked to developed nations, developing economies like India, where the internet and mobile phones are being adopted at much higher rates due to economic stage and population, are also seeing increased data privacy abuse. India has been witnessing a rise in online fraud and cybercrime incidents in recent years, driven by the rapid adoption of digital technologies and internet connectivity. According to the "National Crime Records Bureau (NCRB) Crime in India Report 2020," cybercrime cases registered in India increased by 63.5% in 2020 compared to the previous year. In 2023, as per the data released by NCRB, a total of 11.28 Lakh cases of cybercrimes has been reported.

The Indian government has taken several steps to address cybercrime, including the establishment of cybersecurity agencies like CERT-In and the Cyber Crime Prevention Against Women and Children (CCPWC) initiative. The Information Technology (Amendment) Act, 2008, has been amended to include provisions related to cybercrime and its punishments. The Reserve Bank of India (RBI) and other regulatory bodies have issued guidelines to enhance cybersecurity in the banking and financial sector.

Cybercrime in India is primarily governed by the Information Technology Act, 2000 (IT Act), and its subsequent amendments, along with relevant provisions of the Bharatiya Nyaya Sanhita 2023.

The IT Act grants certain rights to individuals regarding their electronic data and transactions, including the right to secure access to computer resources and the right to privacy. Victims of cybercrime have the right to report the offense to the appropriate authorities and seek redressal.

Some common offenses and their associated penalties under the Information Technology Act 2000 include:

a. **Unauthorized Access and Hacking:** Section 43 of the IT Act deals with unauthorized access to computer systems, computer networks, or computer resources. The punishment includes compensation to the affected person.

b. **Data Theft and Breach of Confidentiality:** Section 43A of the IT Act addresses data theft, unauthorized disclosure of personal information, and breach of confidentiality. The punishment includes compensation to the affected person.

c. **Identity Theft and Impersonation:** Section 66C of the IT Act deals with identity theft and punishment for the fraudulent use of electronic signatures. The punishment includes imprisonment of up to 3 years and/or a fine up to 1 Lakh.

    Section 66D of the IT Act addresses punishment for cheating by personation using a computer resource. The punishment includes imprisonment of up to 3 years and/or a fine up to 1 Lakh.

d. **Cyber and other IT Fraud and Forgery:** Section 66 of the IT Act covers various computer related offences and punishments. The severity of the punishment varies depending on the nature and amount involved in the fraud. The punishment prescribed is imprisonment up to three years and/or fine up to Five Lakh.

Section 336 (read with section 337) and 335 of the Bharatiya Nyaya Sanhita, address forgery and punishment for making a false electronic record or electronic signature. The punishment includes imprisonment and/or a fine.

e. **Cyber Stalking and Harassment:** Section 66E of the IT Act addresses privacy violations and punishment for capturing, publishing, or transmitting the image of a private area of an individual without consent.

Section 78 of the Bharatiya Nyaya Sanhita 2023 (quondam Section 354D of the Indian Penal Code 1860) addresses stalking and punishment for the same.

f. **Cyber Terrorism and Disruption of Services:** Section 66F of the IT Act addresses cyber terrorism, which includes acts that threaten the security, integrity, and sovereignty of India. The punishment includes imprisonment for life and/or a fine.

It's important to note that the specific penalties for each offense may vary based on the severity of the crime and the discretion of the court.

If you have just suffered from an online fraud, here are some steps you can take to mitigate the damage and report the incident:

- Secure Your Accounts by Changing your passwords immediately for the affected accounts and any other accounts that share similar login credentials.

- Take screenshots or gather any relevant documentation, such as emails, transaction records, or chat logs, that can serve as evidence of the fraud.

- If the fraud involves unauthorized transactions on your bank account or credit card, contact your bank or credit card provider immediately. Inform them about the fraudulent activity, provide details of the transactions, and follow their instructions for reporting and resolving the issue.

- File a complaint with your local police or cybercrime cell. Provide them with all the relevant details and evidence you have collected.

The Indian government has also established the National Cyber Crime Reporting Portal (www.cybercrime.gov.in) to enable individuals to report cybercrimes online. It's advisable to know the provisions of the IT Act and other relevant laws or seek legal advice for a comprehensive understanding of the legal rights and punishments for cybercrime in India. Victims of cybercrimes can file a complaint at the nearest police station or approach specialized cybercrime investigation units, such as the Cyber Crime Cells or Cyber Crime Investigation Units in various cities.

Murder, Attempt to Murder & Culpable Homicide

"All attempted murders are not culpable homicide, all culpable homicides are not murder, but all murders are culpable homicide and even an attempted murder is a severe offense."

Chapter VI of the Bharatiya Nyaya Sanhita 2023 (formerly Sections 299 to 377 of the Indian Penal Code 1860) consists of offenses affecting the human body.

Let's understand the basic definitions of these 3 interrelated offenses.

As per Section 100 of the Bharatiya Nyaya Sanhita 2023 (quondam Section 299 of IPC 1860), "Whoever causes death by doing an act with the intention of causing death, or with the intention of causing such bodily injury as is likely to cause death, or with the knowledge that he is likely by such act to cause death, commits the offense of culpable homicide."

Culpable homicide amounting to murder has been dealt with in Section 101 of BNS 2023 (quondam Section 299 of IPC 1860) to mean a situation in which the offense of culpable homicide shall become murder if the following ingredients are present:

- When an act is committed with the intent/desire to kill someone.

- Causing physical harm that the criminal knows would result in death.

- Bodily harm that results in death in the natural course.

- Committing an impending risky act for no valid reason that would result in death or physical damage that would result in death.

The exceptions to Section 101 are as follows, and if proven, the person may not be charged with the offense of murder, though still liable for the criminal offense of culpable homicide:

- Grave and sudden provocation.

- During the exercise of the right of self defense.

- Public servant exercising powers given to him by law.

- Death in a sudden fight, without prior intent.

- Consent of the deceased above the age of 18.

If the culpable homicide does not amount to murder due to the absence of ingredients or the presence of one of the exceptions mentioned under Section 101, then the offense shall be called a culpable homicide not amounting to murder.

Section 103 of the BNS provides that any individual who commits murder shall face either a death sentence or a sentence of imprisonment for life along with a fine. Additionally, it is important to note here that if a group of five or more individuals, commit murder on the grounds of race, caste or community, sex, place of birth, language, personal belief, or any other similar ground, each member of the group shall be subject to either the death penalty or life imprisonment, in addition to a fine. The punishments under this provision are elaborated in detail below:

The court has the discretion to determine the appropriate punishment within the prescribed range of penalties based on the specific circumstances of the case and the severity of the offense.

Section 105 of the BNS 2023 **(Quondam Section 304 of IPC 1860)** addresses the offense of culpable homicide not amounting to murder. It distinguishes cases where death is caused without the intention to cause death but with knowledge that the act is likely to cause death or grievous hurt. Section 105 of BNS 2023 applies when death is caused by a person's act without the intention to cause death. The act is done with the knowledge that it is likely to cause death or cause such bodily injury as is likely to cause death. The act should not be premeditated or intentional but still results in the death of a person. The punishment for culpable homicide not amounting to murder under Section 105, is imprisonment for life or a term which may extend to 10 years but not less than 5 years, along with a possible fine.

Section 106 (quondam Section 304(A) of IPC 1860) - Culpable Homicide by Rash or Negligent Act: Section 106 applies when death is caused by a person's rash or negligent act. The act must be done with the knowledge that it is likely to cause death or cause such bodily injury as is likely to cause death. This section covers cases where death is caused due to the reckless or negligent behavior of a person. The punishment under Section 106 is imprisonment for a term which may extend to maximum 10 years, along with a fine.

It's important to note that the specific circumstances and evidence play a crucial role in determining the charges and subsequent legal proceedings. The interpretation and application of Sections 105 and 106 may vary depending on the facts of each case and the discretion of the court.

Section 109 of the BNS 2023 (quondam Section 307 of IPC 1860) addresses the offense of attempt to murder. It states that whoever does any act with the intention of causing the death of another person, but the act does not result in death, is said to commit the offense of attempt to murder.

The key elements that need to be established to prove an attempt to murder are:

a.   Intention: The accused must have the intention to cause the death of another person.

b.   Act: The accused must perform an act toward causing the death of the intended victim.

c.   Absence of Death: The act should not result in the death of the victim.

Attempt to commit murder is a non-bailable offense and is punishable under Section 109(2) of the BNS 2023. If found guilty, the offender may face imprisonment for a term which can extend up to 10 years and may be liable for a fine. In cases where the court determines that the offense was committed with extreme seriousness, such as premeditated or with the use of lethal weapons, the punishment may extend to imprisonment for life.

As we can see above, the death of a person due to an act by someone may be classified into different sections of BNS. Engaging in physical altercations can dangerously implicate someone and may lead to serious consequences, including charges of murder, attempt to murder, or culpable homicide.

It is always advisable to avoid violence and resolve conflicts through peaceful means. However, if you find yourself in a situation where a physical confrontation is unavoidable, here are some precautions to consider:

- If you need to protect yourself from harm, use only the necessary amount of force required to defend yourself, under the right of self defense.

- Act in proportion to the threat faced and do not escalate the level of violence beyond what is necessary for self-defense.

- Whenever possible, try to retreat from the situation or remove yourself from the scene to avoid further conflict. Escaping from a dangerous situation is often the best course of action to prevent harm to yourself or others.

- If you are involved in a physical altercation, try to attract the attention of others and seek assistance. Contact the police or relevant authorities to report the incident and seek their intervention. It is crucial to maintain a calm demeanour and control your emotions during a fight or confrontation. Acting impulsively and letting anger or frustration guide your actions can lead to severe consequences. Taking precautions and maintaining a non-violent approach can help minimize the risk of serious legal consequences.

- **Avoid using weapons or dangerous objects:** Do not resort to using weapons or any objects that can cause serious harm or escalate the situation, even if you don't intend to use them. Using weapons can significantly increase the legal repercussions and the likelihood of causing severe injury or death.

If possible, try to document the incident by taking photographs, recording videos, or gathering any other evidence that may help establish the facts of the situation. This evidence can be useful in legal proceedings to support your version of events.

If you believe someone has been murdered or there has been an attempted murder, it is essential to contact the appropriate authorities. Immediately call the police or emergency services in your country (100 in India, 911 in the United States, 999 in the United Kingdom, etc.) to report the incident. Provide them with accurate information about the location, nature of the incident, and any details you can provide about the suspect(s). If you are at the crime scene, avoid touching or tampering with any potential evidence. It is crucial to preserve the scene as much as possible until the authorities arrive. This includes not moving or altering any objects or belongings unless necessary for immediate safety.

When the police or law enforcement officials arrive, provide them with all relevant information you have regarding the incident. Cooperate fully and honestly with their investigation, providing any details or descriptions that may assist them in their work.

Remember, every jurisdiction may have specific procedures and protocols for reporting and dealing with incidents of murder or attempted murder. It is important to be vigilant, follow the instructions of the local authorities, and seek legal advice tailored to your specific circumstances.

Defamation, Slander, and Libel

Freedom of speech and opinion may cross a line and become an offense of defamation, slander, and libel. These are among the most frequently contested issues in courts globally and are common subjects of civil suits. Balancing freedom of speech and the protection of reputation is an ongoing challenge, and legal systems strive to strike a balance that upholds both rights.

Even though freedom of speech and opinion are protected rights in many jurisdictions, it is important to understand that this freedom is not absolute and can be subject to certain restrictions to protect the rights and reputation of others.

The exact limits on freedom of speech and the legal consequences of defamation, slander, or libel can vary depending on the jurisdiction. However, here are some general points to consider:

1. False Statements: Defamation, slander, and libel typically involve false statements. If a statement is true, it generally cannot be considered defamatory, as truth is a valid defense against such claims.

2. Harm to Reputation: Defamation, slander, and libel cases require that the false statements harm the reputation of the person or entity targeted. Mere opinions, criticisms, or statements of general dissatisfaction may not necessarily be defamatory.

3. Public Interest and Opinion: The distinction between fact and opinion can be crucial in determining whether a statement is defamatory or not and whether it has been made within the limits of freedom of expression and speech.

4. Dissemination to a third party is an essential component for defamation cases.

5. Legal remedies for defamation can include monetary damages, injunctions, or retractions.

Now, let's understand the genre of these offenses, their rationale, and origin.

Defamation refers to the act of making false statements about someone that harm their reputation. In India, defamation is both a civil wrong and a criminal offense. The provisions related to defamation are primarily covered under the Bharatiya Nyaya Sanhita 2023 and the Civil Law. Criminal defamation is covered under Section 356 of the Bharatiya Nyaya Sanhita 2023. Section 356 defines defamation as making or publishing any imputation concerning a person, intending to harm their reputation, or knowing that it may harm their reputation. BNS under Section 356 prescribes the punishment for defamation, which includes imprisonment for up to 2 years and a fine, or community service.

Civil defamation allows individuals or entities to seek legal remedies and claim compensation for damage to their reputation. The aggrieved party can file a civil suit for defamation seeking monetary damages for the harm caused to their reputation.

To establish defamation, the following elements must be satisfied:

a. The existence of a false statement.

b. The false statement is made about a person or company.

c. The false statement is published or communicated to a third party.

d. The false statement harmed the reputation of the person.

There have been several high-profile defamation cases in India involving individuals from various walks of life, including politicians, public figures, and media organizations. These cases often generate significant public attention and legal scrutiny.

If we analyze the definition of defamation under Section 356 (quondam Section 499 of IPC), we find that the mode of making statements to people at large can be in 2 forms:

1. Making a false statement (spoken) - this part is called slander.

2. Publishing the false statement in writing, printed, or other permanent forms - this part is treated as libel.

So, in India, both slander and libel are covered as one offense, and that is defamation. Other jurisdictions like the USA/UK also have similar definitions of these offenses, but they need to be read with other laws/ regulations. For example, in the USA, the First Amendment of the Constitution preserves freedom of speech rights, and so to succeed in a defamation lawsuit, the plaintiff must demonstrate that the false statement was made with actual malice (knowledge of falsity or reckless disregard for the truth) if they are a public figure or official.

In cases of defamation, including slander (spoken defamation) and libel (written defamation), various defenses may be available depending on the jurisdiction. It's important to note that the availability and requirements of these defenses can vary depending on the specific laws of the country or state where the defamation case is being pursued. Here are some common defenses used in defamation cases:

- Truth or Substantial Truth - A defense commonly available in defamation cases is proving that the statement made is true or substantially true. If the statement can be shown to be substantially true, it may serve as a complete defense against a defamation claim.

- Absolute Privilege - Certain statements made by individuals in specific situations may be protected by absolute privilege. Absolute privilege typically applies to statements made in judicial or legislative proceedings, protecting individuals from defamation claims even if the statements are false or made with malice.

- Qualified Privilege – Qualified privilege may apply in situations where the person making the statement has a legal or moral duty to communicate the information to a specific audience or has a legitimate interest in doing so. This defense is often available for statements made in the public interest or for the protection of one's own interests.

- Fair Comment or Opinion – Statements of pure opinion or fair comment on matters of public interest may be protected as a defense to defamation. However, it is crucial that the statement is presented as an opinion and not as a statement of fact.

- Valid Consent – If the person allegedly defamed consented to the publication of the statement, it can serve as a defense. Consent should be voluntary, informed, and given without any undue influence or coercion or by a minor.

- Innocent Dissemination – In some jurisdictions, individuals or entities that merely distribute or republish defamatory statements without knowledge of their defamatory nature may be protected if they can demonstrate they had no reason to believe the statements were false or could be defamatory.

If someone makes a defamatory statement against you, then you must preserve any evidence related to the defamatory statement and evaluate the statement to determine if it meets the legal criteria for defamation and the harm it may have caused or your contemplation of harm.

Generally, defamation requires a false statement that harms your reputation and is communicated to a third party. You may consider contacting the person who made the defamatory statement, politely expressing your concerns, and requesting that they retract or remove the statement or apologize. If informal communication is ineffective, you should hire an attorney for a cease and desist letter to the offending party, demanding that they stop making or spreading the defamatory statement. This letter may indicate your intent to take legal action if necessary.

Defamation through social media handles is a common issue in today's digital age. If you find yourself facing defamation through social media, here are some steps you can take:

- Take screenshots with relevant details such as the date, time, and the username or profile of the person responsible for the defamatory statement.

- Report the offending content to social media platforms. The platforms generally have reporting mechanisms in place for dealing with abusive or defamatory content. Report the defamatory posts to the respective social media platform. Provide them with the necessary information and evidence to support your claim. The platform may take action by removing the content or suspending the account.

- Respond promptly and respectfully: Depending on the severity of the defamation and the potential impact on your reputation, you may consider responding to the defamatory statement in an appropriate, respectful, and measured manner. Provide factual information or a clear rebuttal if appropriate. However, be cautious not to engage in online arguments or escalate the situation further. Again, ask for an apology or retraction of the statement, and if the offender doesn't comply, send a cease and desist order with possible legal consequences.

Social media trolling is another issue that can also lead to defamation cases. Trolling refers to the act of deliberately provoking or harassing individuals online, often with the intent to provoke an emotional response or create disruption. Dealing with social media trolling can be challenging, but you may start by blocking the offenders and reporting them to the social media platforms. You must consider your mental health in all these social media harassment cases and resort to administrative authorities, social media complaint cells, women's cells, or local police or counsellors if the statements and harm go beyond bearable levels.

To avoid any potential legal consequences, always avoid making false statements about individuals or organizations that could harm their reputation, and refrain from engaging in online harassment, including sending abusive messages, threats, or engaging in cyberbullying. You should also avoid sharing personal or private information about others on any public platform. Respect people's privacy rights, and do not engage in hate speech or discriminatory behavior. Avoid making derogatory or offensive comments based on someone's race, ethnicity, religion, gender, sexual orientation, or other protected characteristics. Such actions can be legally actionable and may violate anti-discrimination laws. One may be liable for criminal as well as civil prosecution for statements made to the public through spoken, written, or online means, so be vigilant for your rights and cautious of others' rights.

Conspiracy literally means to conspire, and for that, a conspirator needs a sounding board, which is called a co-conspirator. So when at least 2 or more people agree to do some illegal act or illegally do something even legal, the offense of conspiracy is born. However, a person may be indicted alone for the offense of criminal conspiracy if the other co-conspirators are unknown, missing, or dead.

Before 1913, conspiracy per se was not a crime in India. In 1913, the Criminal Law Amendment Act of 1913 inserted Chapter V-A in the I.P.C., which introduced criminal conspiracy as a punishable offense. The IPC defined criminal conspiracy under Section 120A; now, the Bharatiya Nyaya Sanhita 2023 defines criminal conspiracy under Section 61 as an agreement of 2 or more persons to do or cause to be done:

1. An illegal act (an example is a conspiracy to commit rape)
2. An act that is not illegal (legal) by illegal means (an example is getting a job by bribing a senior officer)

The term "illegal" has been defined to mean everything that is an offense against a state or a person under any of the laws of the land. So both criminal and civil sides are involved in this offense.

The proviso attached to Section 61 of BNS, provides that a mere agreement to commit an offense shall amount to criminal conspiracy, and no overt act is required to be proved. Such an overt act is necessary only when the object of the conspiracy is the commission of an illegal act not amounting to an offense. It is immaterial whether the illegal act is the ultimate object of such agreement or is merely incidental to that object.

The key elements of criminal conspiracy under Section 61 are:

1. Agreement: There must be an agreement between 2 or more individuals. It is not necessary that all the participants in the conspiracy be aware of all the details or specifics of the criminal act. It is sufficient that they agree on the general objective of committing the offense.

2. Illegal Act: The agreement must involve an illegal act, whether as a preparation or ultimate act. The act may either be an offense directly punishable under the BNS 2023 or a punishable offense under any other law.

Section 61(2) of the BNS 2023 (formerly known as 120B of the IPC 1860) provides for the punishment for criminal conspiracy. According to this section, when 2 or more persons are involved in a criminal conspiracy and one or more acts are done in furtherance of that conspiracy, each of the conspirators is liable to be punished with the same punishment as provided for that offense. Section 61(2) reads as follows:

Whoever is a party to a criminal conspiracy,—

(a) to commit an offense punishable with death, imprisonment for life, or rigorous imprisonment for a term of 2 years or upwards, shall, where no express provision is made in this Sanhita for the punishment of such a conspiracy, be punished in the same manner as if he had abetted such an offense;

(b) other than a criminal conspiracy to commit an offense punishable as aforesaid shall be punished with imprisonment of either description for a term not exceeding 6 months, or with fine, or with both.

It's important to note that the offense of criminal conspiracy is distinct from the actual offenses committed as a result of the conspiracy. Each conspirator can be held liable for the conspiracy itself, even if the planned crime is not successfully carried out.

Proving criminal conspiracy in India, as in any jurisdiction, requires presenting evidence that establishes the elements of a conspiracy. It's important to provide corroborating evidence to support the existence of the conspiracy and its elements. This can include documentary evidence, witness testimonies, surveillance footage, financial records, or any other relevant evidence that helps establish the conspiracy and the involvement of the accused individuals. In some cases, an overt act may be required to establish criminal conspiracy. An overt act refers to a physical act or step taken by one of the conspirators in furtherance of the conspiracy, even if the actual crime is not completed. The overt act requirement varies depending on the jurisdiction and the specific laws involved.

For example, in countries like the USA, an agreement coupled with the performance of an overt action constitutes criminal conspiracy.

Once the prosecution has established that a case lies against the accused conspirators, it would then attempt to prove why the other co-conspirator is also liable. If any conspirator makes a statement or does an act in furtherance of the common intention after it was first entertained, the other co-conspirators would be equally liable. It is not mandatory that all the conspirators should know each other or the full plan of the conspiracy. What is required is unity of objective, and the means to achieve that objective could be different. For example, in a case of criminal conspiracy to murder, one conspirator might deceptively invite the victim to a particular location, and this person may not be involved in the physical act of murder, but Section 61(2) punishes these 2 conspirators in the same way.

In India, civil conspiracy (also known as tort of conspiracy) is also a legal concept that relates to civil law rather than criminal law. Civil conspiracy refers to an agreement between 2 or more individuals to commit a wrongful act or to achieve an unlawful objective that results in harm to another person or entity. Unlike criminal conspiracy, civil conspiracy focuses on the civil liability and remedies available to the harmed party. To establish a civil conspiracy in India, certain elements must be proven. These elements typically include:

- An agreement or understanding between 2 or more individuals.

- The agreement must be aimed at committing a wrongful act or achieving an unlawful objective.

- The wrongful act or unlawful objective must result in harm or damage to another person or entity.

- The harmed party must suffer actual damages as a result of the conspiracy.

In civil conspiracy cases, the individuals involved in the conspiracy can be held jointly and severally liable for the harm caused. This means that each conspirator can be held responsible for the entire damage caused by the conspiracy, regardless of their individual level of involvement. The harmed party can seek various remedies in a civil conspiracy case, including compensation for damages, injunctive relief to prevent further harm, and other appropriate remedies as determined by the court.

Unlike criminal conspiracy, where the burden of proof lies with the prosecutor, in civil cases, the burden of proof rests with the party making the claim of civil conspiracy. The harmed party must provide sufficient evidence to demonstrate the existence of an agreement, the wrongful act or objective, and the resulting harm.

If you ever suspect a conspiracy against yourself, you must immediately start saving direct evidence in one form or another and record any circumstantial evidence. Afterward, you should consult an attorney who is an expert in the subject matter.

Fighting a criminal conspiracy case in Indian courts requires careful planning, preparation, and the assistance of a skilled criminal defense advocate. Here are some general steps to consider when defending against a criminal conspiracy case in Indian courts:

1. Engage a Competent Defense advocate: A competent advocate can guide you through the legal process, protect your rights, and build a strong defense strategy.

2. Understand the Charges and Evidence: Gain a thorough understanding of the charges against you and the evidence presented by the prosecution. Your advocate will analyze the evidence, identify any weaknesses or inconsistencies, and assess the strength of the prosecution's case.

3. Gather Evidence and Information: Collect evidence and information that support your alibi. This can include documents, photographs, videos, electronic records, or witness statements that place you at a different location during the time the offense occurred. If possible, you should also identify alibi witnesses who can testify that you were present at a different location during the commission of the offense.

4. Challenge the Admissible Evidence: Your advocate may file motions to challenge the admissibility of certain evidence if there are grounds to do so. This could involve arguing that the evidence was obtained unlawfully or that it lacks authenticity or relevance.

It's important to note that each criminal case is unique, and the defense strategy should be tailored to the specific circumstances and evidence involved. Consulting with a qualified advocate is essential to navigate the legal process effectively and protect your rights.

Sedition

Sedition refers to the act of inciting violence, disorder, or rebellion against the authority of a state or a government authority. It involves conduct or speech that aims to undermine the established order or provoke public unrest and distrust. The concept of sedition is present in various legal systems around the world, including India.

Sedition laws were introduced in 17th century England when legislators believed that all who spoke against the government were traitors and should be punished. The law was originally drafted in 1837 by Thomas Macaulay, the British historian-politician.

To my surprise, even though the Indian Penal Code was enacted for India (a British colony then) in 1860, it originally did not include sedition laws under the IPC. Section 124A was inserted in 1870 by an amendment, and sedition became a crime under Section 124A of the Indian Penal Code (IPC). Presently, the Bharatiya Nyaya Samhita 2023 does away with the concept of sedition altogether. This is a significant change from the previous Indian Penal Code (IPC). Previously, Section 124A of the IPC dealt with sedition, criminalizing the acts, that incited hatred or disaffection toward the government. The BNS takes a different approach:

It has introduced offense under Section 147 to Section 158, as offences against the state. Section 152, titled "Act endangering sovereignty, unity, and integrity of India." More particularly talks about sedition. The provision penalizes actions that:

- Advocate secession, armed rebellion, or subversive activities.

- Encourage feelings of separatism.

- Put the sovereignty or unity of India at risk.

As per National Crime Records Bureau (NCRB) reports, Assam recorded the most number of sedition cases in the country in the last 8 years. Out of 475 sedition cases registered in the country between 2014 and 2021, Assam accounted for 69 cases (14.52%). After Assam, the most number of such cases were reported from Haryana (42 cases), followed by Jharkhand (40), Karnataka (38), Andhra Pradesh (32), and Jammu and Kashmir (29).

The objective of such laws is to protect the national integrity and security of the country and prevent major offenses like terrorism or government coups.

It's important to note that the interpretation and application of Section 152 can vary, and the indictment of charges has been a subject of debate in India. Critics argue that the law is vaguely worded and can be used to stifle dissent and curtail freedom of expression. In recent years, there have been calls for reform or repeal of the sedition law.

Some of the concerns raised about sedition laws include:

- Chilling Effect: The existence of sedition laws can create a chilling effect, causing individuals to self-censor or refrain from expressing their views due to fear of potential legal consequences. This can restrict the free flow of ideas, public discourse, and the ability to hold governments accountable.

- Vagueness and Overbreadth: Critics argue that sedition laws, in some cases, have vague and overbroad language, which can be open to interpretation and misuse. The lack of clarity about what constitutes seditious speech or acts can lead to subjective enforcement and potential infringement on legitimate expressions of dissent or criticism.

- Silencing Dissent: There are concerns that sedition laws can be used to silence political opponents, activists, journalists, or individuals expressing dissenting opinions. The fear of being charged with sedition may deter individuals from engaging in peaceful protests, criticizing policies, or expressing opinions that challenge the status quo.

- International Human Rights Standards: One may argue that sedition laws in certain cases may not conform to international human rights standards, including the right to freedom of expression. International bodies such as the United Nations have emphasized the importance of protecting freedom of expression and have expressed concerns about the misuse of sedition laws to restrict it.

The incitement of violence or public disorder is a constituting element of sedition charges. It is necessary for the act of sedition to cause, or be likely to cause, violence or public disorder, and a reasonable nexus connecting the alleged seditious material and the violence or disorder must be established.

It must also be noted that sedition charges can be framed only when something is done against the establishment and not just against a political party, an association, or even an officer of the government or armed forces.

If you ever face these charges, make sure to have the best advocate deployed to defend yourself. The Constitution of India guarantees the right to freedom of speech and expression under Article 19(1)(a). However, this right is not absolute and is subject to reasonable restrictions mentioned in Article 19(2), which includes matters of public order, incitement to an offense, and sovereignty and integrity of India.

Additionally, various legal defenses or exceptions may be applicable in specific circumstances to counter a charge of sedition. These may include:

1. Truth as a Defense: If the alleged statement or act falls within the ambit of truth or is supported by sufficient evidence, it may be considered a defense in some cases. However, the burden of proving the truth rests on the accused.

2. Lack of Intent: If the accused can establish that their statement or act was not intended to incite violence, hatred, or disaffection against the government or public order, it may be a viable defense.

3. Public Interest: In certain cases, if the alleged statement or act is in the public interest, serves a legitimate purpose, or contributes to constructive criticism or debate, it may be a relevant factor in defense.

4. Constitutional Validity: The constitutionality of Section 152 (erstwhile 124A of IPC), itself can be challenged on the grounds that it violates the fundamental right to freedom of speech and expression. Courts have the power to strike down or interpret laws in a manner consistent with the Constitution.

5. Claiming the Explanation Provided in Section 152 and merits of judicial precedents of high courts/supreme court for indictment of sedition charges. The comments expressing disapprobation of measures of the government with a view to obtaining alteration by lawful means or administrative or other actions of the government, provided that the comment doesn't excite or attempt to excite hatred, contempt, or disaffection, shall not amount to sedition.

In a modern democracy, opposition, dissent, criticism, and protests are important to keep the government accountable to the public at large and act within the parameters of the constitution and laws made thereunder. The exercise of freedom of speech and expression is to be guaranteed by a democratic government, especially when it is exercised against the government itself. Sedition was introduced by the British pre-independence and was given a constitutional validity in 1951 through the First Amendment of the Constitution, where the reasonableness of restriction was introduced. Later, Section 124A was made a cognizable and non-bailable offense in 1973. Now, the section also needs to be read in conjunction with abetment and criminal conspiracy.

In the landmark judgment in the matter of Kedarnath Singh v. State of Bihar (1962), the Supreme Court of India upheld the constitutional validity of section 124A. However, the Court made a key addition to the law of sedition. Following the Federal Court's interpretation, it held that sedition can only be valid if it intends to incite violence. The Court also published guidelines to be followed in the application of Section 124A. However, the misuse of these charges has forced the Hon. Supreme Court to put the section under abeyance in another landmark judgment in 2022 in the case of S. G. Vombatkere v. Union of India. Now the union government needs to re-examine the need and use of Section 124A and its possible misuse as a criminal offense against people who may have different views. For now, all the cases are on hold, and one can seek court relief if any FIR is filed for sedition against them.

It's important to note that opinions on sedition laws vary, and there are arguments made in favor of their existence as well. Proponents of sedition laws often argue that they are necessary to safeguard national security, public order, and prevent incitement to violence or armed rebellion. Ultimately, the balance between protecting freedom of speech and expression and maintaining public order and national security is a complex and evolving issue that requires righteous consideration and consistent dialogue.

The Bharatiya Nyaya Sanhita's (BNS) Section 152 marks a shift from the controversial sedition law previously enshrined in the Indian Penal Code (IPC). While both aim to protect India's sovereignty and integrity, Section 152 offers a more targeted approach. The BNS moves beyond the ambiguity of "sedition" by focusing on specific actions. It criminalizes acts that directly threaten national unity, such as advocating for secession or inciting armed rebellion. This clarity offers a more precise legal framework for addressing genuine threats. However, Terms like "subversive activities" lack clear definition, potentially leading to subjective interpretations. This creates the risk of stifling legitimate dissent and criticism, a cornerstone of a healthy democracy. The BNS's approach represents a step toward a more balanced legal framework. However, to truly safeguard both national security and freedom of expression, a more precise definition of key terms of Section 152, is very crucial. This will ensure clarity for law enforcement and protect the fundamental right to dissent. Only then can the BNS fulfill its promise of safeguarding India's unity without compromising the voices of its citizens.

Consumer Protection and Warranty

The word "consumer" is derived from the Latin verb "consumere," which combines "con-" and "sumere." In Latin, "consumere" meant "to use up, eat, waste, or destroy."

The concept of consumer protection has evolved over centuries, reflecting changes in society, economy, and technology. Consumer protection can be traced back to ancient civilizations. For example, the Code of Hammurabi (circa 1754 BC) in Babylon included laws that protected consumers against unfair trade practices. In the early modern period, the regulation of the market and the Industrial Revolution during the 18th and 19th centuries brought significant changes in production safety and consumption guidelines.

After World War II, consumer protection became a more prominent issue. The establishment of organizations like the United Nations and country like the United States outlined 4 basic consumer rights: the right to safety, the right to be informed, the right to choose, and the right to be heard. These principles became the foundation for modern consumer protection laws.

The late 20th and early 21st centuries saw the rise of globalization and the digital economy, bringing new challenges and opportunities for consumer protection. Issues like data privacy, e-commerce fraud, and international trade practices required new approaches and regulations. Consumer protection has increasingly become a global issue, with international trade & cooperation and such agreements playing a key role. Organizations like the International Consumer Protection and Enforcement Network

(ICPEN) and guidelines from bodies like the OECD help harmonize consumer protection standards across countries.

Consumer protection in India is governed by a robust legal framework aimed at safeguarding the rights and interests of consumers. Now, let's delve into the consumer protection situation in India, which is being managed through the Consumer Protection Act 2019. This act, inter alia, gives the following 6 rights to consumers:

1. The right to be protected against the marketing of goods and services which are hazardous to life and property.

2. The right to be informed about the quality, quantity, potency, purity, standard, and price of goods or services.

3. The right to be assured of access to a variety of goods or services at competitive prices.

4. The right to be heard and to be assured that consumer interests will receive due consideration.

5. The right to seek redressal against unfair or restrictive trade practices.

6. The right to consumer education.

One of the key features of the Consumer Protection Act, 2019 is the establishment of Consumer Protection Councils and Consumer Dispute Redressal Commissions (CDRCs). These bodies have been empowered to handle disputes and ensure justice for consumers.

The Act includes specific provisions to address issues related to e-commerce, including the requirement for e-commerce entities to acknowledge consumer complaints within 48 hours and resolve them within one month. Manufacturers, service providers, and sellers have been made liable to compensate consumers for any harm caused by defective products or deficient services.

The Act provides for stringent action against misleading advertisements and false claims. Endorsers can also be held liable for endorsing misleading products. The Act defines and prohibits various unfair trade practices to protect consumer interests.

The Act also provides the mechanism for mediation cells attached to the consumer commissions for faster and amicable resolution of disputes.

Warranty as a consumer right is another important aspect of consumer protection laws worldwide as well as in the Consumer Protection Act, 2019. It ensures that consumers receive a product that meets certain standards of quality and performance. A warranty can be an express warranty or an implied warranty. When there is a promise made by the seller or manufacturer about the quality, condition, or performance of a product, and more specifically in writing, we call that an express warranty. The best example is the warranty given on cars or other white goods. On the other hand, implied warranties are not explicitly stated but are legally assumed in any sales transaction about the merchantability/fitness/safety for a particular purpose. For example, when we buy a food product or medicine, there is an implied warranty that the product is not expired. Under warranty, we assume quality assurance as well as a remedy for defects. Warranty gives us trust and confidence in a particular product and service, which ultimately makes them a good, trusted, and reliable brand.

The Consumer Protection Act, 2019 includes provisions for warranties and guarantees, ensuring that consumers can seek redress for defective products and services. It also empowers consumer courts to enforce warranty claims. Warranties play a crucial role in protecting consumers by ensuring that products meet certain standards and providing remedies when they do not. As a consumer right, warranties enhance consumer confidence, promote fair trade practices, and provide legal protection against defective products. Understanding the terms and conditions of warranties and knowing how to enforce them is essential for consumers to fully exercise their rights.

The Central Consumer Protection Authority (CCPA) is a regulatory authority established to promote, protect, and enforce the rights of consumers. It can take suo motu actions, recall products, order refunds, and impose penalties for misleading advertisements.

In situations where you have been cheated on the quality of a product or deficiency in services, you must know your legal rights and the appropriate forum for the redressal of your grievances. In general, please note the following important points:

1. Collect all necessary documents such as purchase receipts, invoices, warranty cards, and any correspondence with the seller or service provider.

2. Contact the seller or service provider to try to resolve the issue directly.

3. Keep a record of all communications, including emails, letters, and phone calls.

4. If the issue is not resolved, draft a formal complaint.

5. The complaint should include your name, address, and contact details, as well as a detailed description of the complaint and the relief sought.

6. Use consumer helplines or online portals to seek guidance. The National Consumer Helpline (NCH) can be reached at 1800-11-4000 or 1915.

7. If the complaint still remains unresolved or you are not happy with the resolution, then you can file formal complaints in the following

forums based on the value of goods or services and the compensation claimed:

- ○ **District Consumer Dispute Redressal Commission:** For cases where the value of goods/services and the compensation claimed does not exceed ₹ 50 lakh.

- ○ **State Consumer Dispute Redressal Commission:** For cases where the value exceeds ₹ 50 lakh but does not exceed ₹ 2 crore.

- ○ **National Consumer Dispute Redressal Commission:** For cases where the value exceeds ₹ 2 crore.

You can also register your complaint online at https://consumerhelpline. gov.in/ The government has launched the **E-Daakhil portal,** allowing consumers to file complaints online at https://edaakhil.nic.in/

You need to keep one factor in mind while making a complaint: the seller might take recourse to the principle of "Caveat Emptor" or "Buyer Beware," wherein it is expected from you to see and inspect the product/ services yourself before transacting. The principle of "buyer beware" can be misused to exploit consumers, leading to unfair practices and market inefficiencies. Examples of misuse of "Buyer Beware" can include hiding facts, writing disclaimers in very small or technical language, misleading advertising, using last-minute or hard-pressed sales pitches, or simply not having a return/refund/redressal policy.

Under the doctrine of caveat emptor as per Section 16 of the Sale of Goods Act, when a product is sold under a contract of sale, the law does not presume that the seller sold it under an implied warranty of fitness and quality. However, there are exceptions to it. One such landmark judgment can be seen in M/S Indsil Hydro Power and Manganese Limited v. State of Kerala and Ors. (2021), where the Supreme Court observed that dotted line commercial contracts are unreasonable and do not form a fair bargain. In another case showing a shift from the strict interpretation of caveat emptor, the Allahabad High Court held in Smt. Rekha Sahu vs. The Uco Bank (2013) that Indian jurisprudence has witnessed a shift from the doctrine of "caveat emptor" to the doctrine of "caveat venditor," where the onus has shifted to sellers to check the product's merchantability and the claims made during the sale. In this case, it was an auction of a land parcel with some electricity dues, and the auctioneers were held liable, as seller.

Road Accident and Negligent Driving

Safe mobility is a crucial aspect of the universal right to health, a fundamental right of every human. Mobility must not, and need not, come with a tragic cost in human lives. The Global Status Report on Road Safety 2023 by the World Health Organization shows that the number of annual road traffic deaths is approximately 1.19 million. The report shows that efforts to improve road safety are having an impact but at a slow pace (in the 2010 report, 1.25 million deaths on the road were recorded).

More than half of the fatalities occur among pedestrians, cyclists, and motorcyclists, particularly those living in low and middle-income countries. Most countries recognize this, but as of now, only 47 countries have policies to promote walking, cycling, and public transport. India's urban transport policies are gradually shifting focus toward creating safer, more accessible environments for pedestrians and cyclists while improving public transport systems. For example, national policies like the Jawaharlal Nehru National Urban Renewal Mission (JNNURM), Atal Mission for Rejuvenation and Urban Transformation (AMRUT), and Smart Cities Mission (SCM) are focused on improving the infrastructure to promote safe passage for walking and cycling. However, in general, the focus has moved to mass transit in all these central plans.

It is encouraging to see city-level initiatives like:

1. Chennai city has drafted non-motorized transport policies to create footpaths along 80% of its streets and prioritize people over vehicles. This includes infrastructure like cycle lanes to improve safety and accessibility.

2. Pimpri Chinchwad city adopted a Non-Motorized Transport Policy in 2022, aiming to have 90% of trips made by public transport, walking, or cycling by 2036. The policy focuses on creating a safe and seamless network for pedestrians and cyclists and integrates sustainable environmental planning.

3. Coimbatore city has implemented a Street Design & Management Policy to prioritize NMT and public transport in urban planning, design, and budgeting.

4. Mysuru city has implemented public bicycle-sharing systems, and initiatives like India Cycles4Change are prioritizing streets for pedestrians and cyclists.

Preliminary data available as of now indicates that road accidents remain a critical public safety issue in India, with approximately 168,491 deaths reported in 2022, reflecting a troubling increase in fatalities from previous years. We don't have data for 2023 as of now, which shows the seriousness and preparedness of the system to track and effectively control road accidents. The Indian government has been working on a multi-faceted strategy to reduce road accidents, focusing on the "4Es" of road safety: Education, Engineering, Enforcement, and Emergency Care. Initiatives such as road safety audits, implementation of modern transportation systems, and international collaborations are part of this strategy. Additionally, the use of technology like Electronic Detailed Accident Reports (e-DAR) for real-time data analysis is being promoted to address the issue more effectively. We hope that our country becomes accident-free soon, and so does the world.

Now let's talk about the enforcement part and the laws of the land and mechanism of enforcement of traffic laws and punitive provisions in India.

Under the old Indian Penal Code (IPC), several provisions address negligent driving and related offenses:

Section 304A - Causing Death by Negligence: This section deals with causing death by doing any rash or negligent act not amounting to culpable homicide. It is commonly used in cases involving negligent driving that results in death. The punishment prescribed is imprisonment for up to 2 years, or a fine, or both.

Section 279 - This section specifically addresses rash driving or riding on a public way. It penalizes any person who drives or rides any vehicle on a public way in a manner that is rash or negligent and endangers human life or is likely to cause hurt or injury to any other person. The punishment is imprisonment of either description for a term that may extend to 6 months, or with a fine that may extend to one thousand rupees, or with both.

Section 337 - This section deals with causing hurt to any person by doing any act so rashly or negligently as to endanger human life or the personal safety of others. The punishment is imprisonment for a term that may extend to 6 months, or with a fine that may extend to 5 hundred rupees, or with both.

Section 338 - This section addresses causing grievous hurt to any person by doing any act so rashly or negligently as to endanger human life or the personal safety of others. The punishment is imprisonment of either description for a term that may extend to 2 years, or with a fine that may extend to one thousand rupees, or with both.

Now, the Bharatiya Nyaya Sanhita (BNS) includes specific provisions for hit-and-run cases causing death, contained in Section 106. This section has 2 main provisions:

1. **General Negligence:** If a person causes death by any rash or negligent act that does not amount to culpable homicide, they can be punished with imprisonment of up to 5 years and a fine.

2. **Negligent Driving and Hit-and-Run:** If a person causes death by rash and negligent driving and escapes without reporting to the police or a magistrate, they can be punished with imprisonment of up to 10 years and a fine.

The new Bharatiya Nyaya Sanhita (BNS), which came into effect on July 1, 2024, includes specific provisions for road accidents, particularly focusing on hit-and-run cases. The introduction of these provisions has led to significant protests by truck and bus drivers across various states, who argue that the penalties are too harsh and were implemented without sufficient consultation of stakeholder.

Section 106(2) of the Bharatiya Nyaya Sanhita, which prescribes a 10-year imprisonment along with fine, for hit-and-run cases, has been put on hold for execution and hence, for the time being, such cases shall be handled under Section 106(1), which has milder punishment. The new laws also provide some leniency if the driver involved in the accident promptly reports the incident to the police or transports the victim to the nearest hospital. In such cases, the driver may not face charges/severe charges, emphasizing the importance of immediate assistance to the victims.

However, looking at the Supreme Court judgment last year on 28th March 2023 in State of Punjab v. Dil Bahadur, 2023, SC Cr. Apl 844/2023, the Hon. Supreme Court quashed the order of the Punjab and Haryana High Court, which reduced the sentence to 8 months from the initial punishment of 2 years on the ground of misplaced sympathy, taking note of the payment made to the victim's family. The Supreme Court emphasized that appropriate punishment should be awarded in such cases to deter similar conduct by others in society.

Key factors in determining rashness or negligence include the width of the road, traffic density, attempts to overtake other vehicles, and driving on the wrong side of the road, as elucidated in Shakila Khader v. Naushe

Gama, AIR 1975 SC 1324. An error of judgment on the part of the driver does not constitute liability under Section 304A. For instance, in a scenario where a bus driver, traveling at a moderate speed, suddenly notices a child attempting to cross the road and diverges to the extreme right to avoid the child, resulting in a fatal collision, the driver's action would be considered an error of judgment rather than negligence (also see Syed Akbar v. State of Karnataka, 1979 Cr LJ 1375).

Similarly, the Supreme Court in Mohd. Aynuddin v. State of Andhra Pradesh, 2000 Cr LJ 3508 held that merely because a passenger fell from the bus while boarding it and died, the presumption of negligence cannot be drawn against the bus driver. The death must be the direct result of the rash or negligent act of the accused, and the act must be a sufficient cause.

The Court has also highlighted the dangers of rash and negligent driving, especially under the influence of alcohol, and the need for stringent punishment to serve as a deterrent. While the act may not be intentional, the gross negligence and recklessness exhibited by the accused amount to culpable homicide not amounting to murder.

If you are unfortunately involved in a road accident, it is essential to follow a calm approach. First, assess the situation and check for any injuries. Evaluate the safety of the scene, and if there are any immediate dangers, such as fire or traffic, take steps to minimize them. If someone is injured, immediately provide first aid and dial emergency numbers, followed by reporting the incident to the police. Do not approach the other party in anger or accept fault on the spot. It is also advisable to document the scene by taking videos/photos of the vehicle number and any other relevant evidence, such as an eyewitness or traffic signal, and fully cooperate with the police and medical professionals. By following these steps, you can ensure that you handle the situation effectively, provide necessary assistance, and comply with legal requirements.

SECTION 4

MEN'S RIGHTS IN INDIA

A brief thought on the specific right which are available or should be made available for men who suffers the misuse of strict and unilateral protection given to females under our legislature and judicial system.

The Constitution of India is founded on the principle of equality, a cornerstone for fostering societal development and justice. As I endeavor to write about a topic that, while rooted in factual reality, may appear to lean in favor of men, I am conscious of the potential for it to be perceived as controversial. This unease stems from the delicate balance needed when addressing issues of gender, where interpretations can easily vary. My intention is to present a fair and accurate perspective, yet I am mindful of how such discussions can evoke diverse reactions, particularly when they touch on gender dynamics.. There is no national men's cell like we have a national women's cell, and even at the international level, we don't have a UN Commission on Men's Rights despite International Men's Day being celebrated on November 19th. Despite demands since the 1960s, International Men's Day was finally inaugurated in 1992 by Thomas Oaster in Malta.

Do you know what the theme of International Men's Day has been since 2023 and now in 2024? It is very surprising and rather shocking: **"Zero Male Suicide."**

For decades, it has been depicted through mythologies, literature, and other forms of expression that women are inferior and men are superior. This is the very foundation of today's reality, where reservations are sought for women, from public transport to parliament. Men are supposed to be powerful and aggressive, while women are perceived as oppressed and silent sufferers of all forms of violence, even to the extent of ignoring their victimization in this false sense of superiority. Men can face social stigma when making complaints against their counterparts, for their perceived lack of masculine machismo and the fear of not being believed by authorities. Please realise and accept that a masculine gender too can have problem and can be in pain *"Mard ko Bhi Dard Hota Hai"*

Whether you agree with this perspective or not, I'll leave that decision to you. My aim here isn't to influence your opinion but rather to present some facts and offer guidance if you find yourself facing unfounded and uncomfortable accusations, feeling unfairly targeted. In my personal opinion, to reach true gender equality, it's essential to recognize that advocating for men's rights doesn't mean diminishing the importance of women's rights. Moreover, it's vital to approach these discussions with empathy, understanding, and a commitment to inclusivity, acknowledging that both men and women can face unique challenges and injustices based on their gender.

While I deeply empathize with the necessity of ensuring that our mothers, sisters, and daughters are protected from harm at all costs, there are situations where, in the heat of the moment, a serious complaint may be lodged over relatively minor issues without fully considering the long-term consequences. For a man who values his self-respect and dignity, such an accusation can have a profound impact, even if the court ultimately rules in his favor. The emotional and reputational toll of being subjected to such a serious allegation can extend far beyond the legal verdict, affecting one's sense of self respect and standing in the community.

Men's rights advocacy often focuses on areas where there is perceived inequality or discrimination against men, such as in family law, custody rights, paternity leave, and societal expectations around masculinity. These discussions aim  to address issues like the gender pay gap, access to healthcare, mental health support, and representation in certain professions. Women, like men, are human beings with the full spectrum of capabilities, including the potential to misuse power. Unfortunately, this can sometimes result in situations where a woman's actions might severely impact a man's life—not necessarily through physical harm, but certainly through emotional and mental distress. Additionally, it is important to recognize that both men and women are equally capable of instigating violence against one another. Gender does not exempt one from accountability, nor does it inherently protect one from the consequences of actions that can harm others. This understanding is crucial in addressing issues of fairness and justice in all interpersonal relationships.

Since a court cannot pronounce anyone's guilt or liability without evidence, it can be safely said that the Bharatiya Sakhsya Adhiniyam 2023 (formerly The Indian Evidence Act) is the most important law men should be aware of. Everything else—the counter-filed police complaint, vague allegations, false jewelry lists, and tears in the courtroom—might have some sympathy or drama value, but they have zero value in terms of evidence.

In trials, only the evidence, whether documentary or statements by witnesses, matters and not the emotions and feelings. Assuming, of course, that one is hiring a competent advocate to do cross-examination, file documents, etc., at the right times and in an appropriate manner.

One of the significant challenges faced by those accused in such cases is their lack of understanding regarding the nature and importance of evidence. Many do not have even a basic grasp of what constitutes strong versus weak evidence, and this ignorance severely hampers their ability to build a solid defense. Overwhelmed by emotions, they often struggle to think clearly and fail to collect and present the necessary evidence to the court in a timely manner.

Another critical issue is the reliance on legal counsel without fully understanding the importance of active participation in their defense. Many accused individuals assume that hiring a lawyer means they can step back and legal expert shall handle everything. However, without providing substantial evidence, even the most skilled lawyer is reduced to a mere procedural agent, filing petitions, submitting statements, and performing routine cross-examinations. This approach leaves them ill-equipped to effectively challenge and dismantle false accusations made by the opposing party. In such cases, the lack of proactive evidence collection and submission can mean the difference between a successful defense and one that fails to protect the accused's rights and interests.

Now, what is evidence and what is not? For example, a wife's preposterous allegations and a false list of 'dowry' in the CAW cell are not really any evidence. But many husbands get floored at that first hurdle itself and readily move toward the C-word called Compromise. Photocopies of documents are not acceptable as evidence, but they can still be used in cross-examination of the opponent and, based on the situation can be useful to elicit useful points in one's favor. So, one need not lose heart if one doesn't have original documents for everything.

Audio recordings are admissible as evidence. If the opponent's lawyer objects, they can go for voice samples and authentication, but audio recordings can't be dismissed outright. This is another myth being spread by lawyers that audio recordings won't work in court. Maybe the problem is by few laziness, lack of application, and lack of enthusiasm for fighting the husband's case, so he can be steered toward the C-word. To some extent, even the public is to be blamed for unquestioningly believing their lawyers, with eyes shut, which go against common sense.

Relying on neighbors' verbal statements as witnesses might seem like a good idea, especially if they actually saw what happened. However, in the reality of a courtroom, documentary evidence tends to be much more reliable. This is because trials can stretch over long periods, and there's no certainty that your witness will still be available or willing to testify when the time comes—whether that's two years from now or even later. People move, their memories fade, and their willingness to get involved might diminish, especially when they were never truly aware of the full situation.

Moreover, witnesses might hesitate to take a stand due to the moral complexities of the situation, or simply because they don't really know what goes on behind closed doors. It's similar to how we often present a happy, polished version of our lives on social media—even if things are far from perfect in reality.

In light of these uncertainties, gathering documentary evidence—like written records, photos, or videos—becomes crucial. Unlike personal testimonies, these pieces of evidence don't change over time and are less likely to be contested. So, while witness statements can be helpful, having solid, tangible evidence is often what truly strengthens a case in court.

If you're falsely accused of domestic violence and cruelty by your wife and are seeking evidence to defend yourself, it's crucial to approach the situation with care and diligence. Here are some steps you might consider:

- Collect Documentation: Collect any evidence that contradicts the accusations made against you. This could include text messages, emails, or other communications that demonstrate a different narrative or provide an alibi for your whereabouts during the alleged incidents.

- Testimony: If there were witnesses to the events in question, such as family members, friends, or neighbors, their testimony could be valuable in supporting your case. Ask them if they are willing to provide statements or testify in your favor.

- Medical Records: If physical altercations were alleged, medical records could provide evidence of any injuries sustained by either party. Additionally, medical professionals may be able to provide expert testimony regarding the nature and likely causes of any injuries.

- Electronic Evidence: Electronic evidence such as surveillance footage, phone records, or GPS data can help establish true facts or provide context for the events in question. If you feel that you are on the right side of the law but your spouse might frame you in a false case, consider options like phone recording, keeping a camera at home, talking in front of a probable witness, counseling through both parents, and maybe recording, etc.

- File a case of criminal intimidation and breach of trust (section 316, 351 of BNS 2023 and erstwhile section 506/120B of IPC).

- File a suit for restitution of conjugal rights under section 9 of The Hindu Marriage Act.

- Take guidance from the NGO and their expert views.

- Take anticipatory bail if the FIR has been filed and you have not filed for quashing of the FIR.

- File a suit for defamation.

- File a suit for divorce on the grounds of cruelty or other grounds.

It's important to approach the situation sensitively and prioritize your well-being, as well as that of any children involved. False accusations of domestic violence can have serious consequences, so it's crucial to take the necessary steps to defend yourself and protect your rights. You should not hesitate to take action, and if necessary, be proactive in filing a police complaint first. If you find yourself facing a situation where there's a blatant misuse of power against you, it's important to stand your ground. In such cases, you might also consider using social media to raise awareness and to escalate your complaint to higher authorities, such as the commissioner's office. Taking these steps can help ensure that your concerns are addressed and that you receive the protection and justice you deserve.

For **corporate offices and harassment cases**, seriously consider your HR department as the first line of defense, if you are not in the wrong. There could be situations where you really didn't mean to do any harm, but there is an error of interpretation. Simply try to clarify, and there is no shame in saying sorry if the other person interpreted any incident in the wrong perspective.

Without mentioning a generalized case, I will share 2 examples that happened in my life where an error of interpretation occurred, and I was targeted for wrongdoing.

1. During my corporate life as one of the CXOs, I used to admire the working style and work-life balance of one of my female colleagues. One day, I shared that with her with the sheer intent of appreciating her way of life/work and her always being a happy soul, spreading happiness with her positive aura. She thanked me for my statements, but later I learned through one of my seniors that she tried pulling a case against me, alleging that I was trying to disrespect and flirt with her. As I was in a senior position and she was a junior, this might have really gone against me. However, to avoid any such wrong feelings and save myself from allegations, I stopped dealing with that particular department and person, and placed a female staff member from my department to handle those affairs.

2. During my entrepreneurship, when I was having my office at a co-working space, I collided with a lady while entering the elevator. As a courtesy, I said, "Sorry." My apology gave her the confirmation that I did try to touch her intentionally, and then the whole drama ensued, with security guards from the building intervening. Fortunately, the building had a digital camera that captured this unfortunate incident. Upon reviewing the footage, it was revealed that this lady was drunk, and while coming from her cabin to the elevator, she had already experienced two similar incidents of collision but decided not to take them seriously. It was my bad day, and I was really worried about such an allegation/defamation because I had a very good image in that office.

What these incidents teach us is that there are always protections and safety measures available, and it's crucial to explore and utilize them before situations spiral out of control. To help prevent cases of misinterpretation and wrongful accusations, I suggest the following:

- Avoid the situation by being extra vigilant around you.

- Weigh your statements to any female before you make them. It doesn't matter what you may feel inside your heart, but how you get perceived does.

- Apologize gently without protest, saying you didn't mean to offend if she is hurt.

- Open your mind and look at all possible digital/non-digital instruments and people around, like eyewitnesses, your own colleague, guards, cameras, etc., for possible alibis.

Laws and Judicial Precedents

Previously, under Section 498A and/or 406 of the IPC, the focus was primarily on cruelty by a husband or his relatives toward the wife, often within the context of marriage. Now, in the Bharathiya Nyaya Samhita 2023, Sections 85 and 86 expand upon this concept, recognizing the broader spectrum of domestic relationships and the diverse forms of cruelty and harassment that individuals may face. Section 85 encompasses acts of cruelty against women within domestic relationships, extending beyond marriage ties. It now includes all conduct likely to drive the woman to commit suicide or cause grave injury, as well as harassment aimed at coercing her or her relatives to meet unlawful demands.

Over the years, Section 498A has acquired the reputation of being the "most abused law in the history of Indian jurisprudence." With cases of divorce in India steadily rising, campaigners say that disgruntled women, aided by their lawyers, routinely misuse the law to harass their husbands and relatives. It has also been questioned by the Supreme Court, with a judge describing its misuse as "legal terrorism," warning that it was "intended to be used as a shield and not as an assassin's weapon," (*Sushil Kumar Sharma v. Union of India* (2005). Even the National Commission for Women expressed concerns over its misuse but this judgement was protested a lot by various NGO/Feminists for alleged patriarchist benevolence.

The conviction rate for cases filed under Section 498A of the Indian Penal Code, which deals with cruelty by a husband or his relatives towards a woman, has indeed been consistently low over the years. In 2018, the conviction rate for these cases was approximately 13%, significantly lower than the average conviction rate of around 40% for other offenses under the Indian Penal Code (IPC) 1860. This stark difference in conviction rates suggests that a substantial number of Section 498A cases may be based on vague or baseless allegations, leading to a high rate of acquittals.

This low conviction rate raises concerns about the misuse of Section 498A, which was originally designed to protect women from domestic violence and cruelty. While the provision is essential for safeguarding women's rights, the data indicates that it may sometimes be used to file false FIRs, leading to unwarranted legal battles and emotional distress for the accused. This phenomenon shows the importance of ensuring that allegations are thoroughly investigated and substantiated before proceeding with prosecution, to prevent misuse and uphold the integrity of the legal system.

The term "mental cruelty" against a husband has been defined in various contexts, and courts in different judgments have also deliberated that mental cruelty is not a fixed formula applicable to all cases. It refers to the mental anguish a husband experiences when a false case is filed against him, his parents, or his relatives. The word "cruelty" under Section 13(1)(ia) of the Hindu Marriage Act, 1955, has not been defined, making the Court's task more challenging. Cruelty can be physical, mental, or both. While physical cruelty can be corroborated with medical record and other evidences, there is no standard yardstick to assess mental cruelty. The scope of interpretation is wide, and there are bound to be several interwoven circumstances that need to be carefully considered to assess the element of mental cruelty.

Followings are a few landmark judgement to refer wherein the courts perceived the issue in different paradigm.

1.   **Monju Roy v. State of West Bengal, 2015 SCC OnLine SC 358:** The Supreme Court held that brothers and sisters do not stand on the same footing as the husband or parents and should be treated according to available evidence, not merely as parties.

2.   **Sushil Kumar Sharma v. Union of India (2005):** In this landmark case, the Supreme Court acknowledged the misuse of Section 498A, terming it "legal terrorism." The Court highlighted the need for guidelines to prevent frivolous complaints and arrests.

3.   **Safiya Bano Alias Shakira vs. The State Of U.P., 2024:** The Supreme Court accepted the appeal, holding that the change of mind to not honor the settlement and all sections being applied against the husband and his relatives is not sustainable, and the wife's intent was more of a counter-case rather than any case of cruelty.

4.   **Samar Ghosh vs. Jaya Ghosh, SC 2007:** The Hon. Supreme Court, reversing the High Court order and agreeing with the ADJ decision, concluded that mental cruelty occurred on grounds such as the wife's refusal to cohabit, not wanting children out of wedlock, social humiliation, cooking only for herself, and not taking care of her husband during illness.

5.   **Narendra v. K. Meena (SC 2016):** The Supreme Court of India decided that coercion or forcing the husband to leave his parents (who are dependent on his income) amounts to cruelty on the wife's part, thus providing a strong ground for divorce under Hindu Law.

6. **Hiral P. Harsora and ors. vs. Kusum Narottamdas Harsora and ors (Civil Appeal No. 10084 of 2016) (arising out of SLP (civil) no. 9132 of 2015):-** Allowed domestic violence complaints against females/minors in households by removing the requirement of "adult male" from the definition of respondent – Supreme Court judgment.

7. **Raj Talreja v. Kavita Talreja:-** In this case, false allegations were made by the wife against the husband. The court held that this amounts to mental cruelty and can be a ground for divorce.

While there are certain directives and judicial precedents that can be relied upon, and the overall the legislature and judiciary have been addressing the misuse of domestic violence and cruelty provisions, it is always better to know your options both in police and court. In many High Court and Supreme Court judgments, it has been directed to the police department not to make immediate and unnecessary arrests. Arresting a person immediately upon filing of an FIR/case is like passing judgment without a trial.

The Indian men's rights movement was started in 1988 by advocate Ram Prakash Chugh to help husbands facing false dowry cases by their wives. Since then, multiple NGOs have been working in this field with the objective of helping people to keep families together. While researching in the public domain, I came across the following NGOs that can be approached in such cases of false victimization:

- All India Front Against Persecution by Wives (Akhil Bhartiya Patni Atyachar Virodhi Morcha)
- MyNation Hope Foundation
- Vaastav Foundation
- Save Indian Family
- Purush Hakka Sanrakshan Samiti

- Gender Human Rights Society
- Sahodar Trust
- Purusha Commission
- Hridaya-Nest of Family Harmony
- Middle East – Men's Right & Justice – UAE-based Group in the GCC Region
- Karnataka Rajya Purushara Rakshana Samithi

While men may seek help from various institutions, my primary objective in addressing this topic in the book is to equip them with the knowledge of what truly matters in court. It's essential for them to understand the critical points that can make a difference in their defense and to be savvy in navigating legal proceedings, especially when facing false or fabricated accusations. By being informed and strategic, they can better protect themselves and ensure that justice is served.